A Western Horseman Book

Colorado Springs, Colorado

WESTERN TRAINING

THEORY & PRACTICE

By Jack Brainard

with Peter Phinny

Edited by Pat Close

Photographs by Darrell Arnold

WESTERN TRAINING
THEORY & PRACTICE

Published by
The Western Horseman, Inc.

3850 North Nevada Avenue
P.O. Box 7980
Colorado Springs, CO 80933-7980

Design, Typography, and Production
Western Horseman
Colorado Springs, Colorado

Printing
Williams Printing
Colorado Springs, Colorado

ISBN 0-911647-16-3

DEDICATION

This book is dedicated to my sons, Zane and Jody.

Jack Brainard

JACK BRAINARD

FOREWORD

Years ago, while growing up during the Depression era, a teen-ager had few options available for fun and entertainment among the social set of his own age. In our corner of South Dakota, the main event was a dance every Saturday night in a small, no-frills country dance hall. The building had a stage for music, a continuous bench around the perimeter of the room, and a huge pot-bellied stove in a back corner for heat on the cold winter nights. The building itself was really just an old shell, but it did have a good floor and I still have fond memories of the place.

I remember standing with a gang of boys around the old stove wishing that I knew how to dance. (How else could a timid teen-ager get close to those cute girls?) I felt shy and awkward, and I doubted that the cute ones would dance with me if I asked them, and I sure didn't want to get turned down. I did have a friend whose sister was older, but an excellent dancer. I asked my friend if he thought she'd show me how to dance. Well, she grabbed me and jerked me out onto the floor and my lessons began. I'll never forget them.

She constantly talked me through the program: "Don't step! Slide your feet. Keep your feet on the floor." Then she would softly kick my foot; "Get that foot back. Now you're going to slide your foot to the left. That's right! Now back two steps. Good! You aren't listening to the music. Get in time with it. You're too stiff. Relax and have fun. Don't try to go too fast until you know where to put your feet. Be graceful. Slide! That's better; listen to the music."

This girl continued to push, pull, slide, direct, tap, and talk me through the moves. I guess I became a pretty good pupil because in a few weeks I was able to dance as well as any of the boys my age, and all the girls were willing to dance when I asked them.

When I thought about this, I realized that I was in exactly the same situation that my colts are in now. I can sure as heck relate to them. They are just like I was when that girl first jerked me out onto the dance floor. This time, however, I'm the teacher and I'm going to try to show them the way. I want them to listen to the music the same way that I had to, to find the beat, move their feet, slide, be graceful, and, above all, relax and have fun. I do know that if I can teach my horses as well as that gal taught me on that old dance floor, I will have it made.

If, in the pages of this book, I can convince a reader or a trainer (and every rider is a trainer) that there is an easy, soft way to train a horse, and that the trainer who uses the least amount of force is the best, then I have at least given that reader or trainer a decent start toward becoming a horseman.

My biggest reward, and the most satisfaction I can get, is in knowing that somewhere within the following pages I have succeeded in preventing a colt from being pulled, jerked, spurred, or abused. If I can convince one trainer to think like a horse, to analyze, to observe, and, above all, to wait patiently for progress, then I will have contributed and that trainer will be much more effective in his chosen profession. I'll guarantee it.

—*Jack Brainard*

PREFACE

Jack Brainard startled me when we first became acquainted. I was a young writer and he an established judge, trainer, and horse breeder. What I had not been prepared for was his depth of knowledge and his voracity for self-improvement. His bookshelves were filled with not only volumes regarding the evolution of horses and of horse training, but also with western American history and with books on individual and personal development. In this latter category his tastes range from *Psycho-Cybernetics* by Maxwell Maltz to vocabulary development books.

After Jack's lifetime in close contact with horses, the theories that he has come to embrace for the process of training a western horse are surprisingly sensible, and ultimately attainable. Some trainers speak as if training horses is somehow a magical process; Jack does not. He, on the other hand, continually builds confidence in our potential as humans to relate to our horses, realizing that developing a well-trained horse, like a skilled baseball player, requires good communication skills. This book deals with developing communication skills as much as it does with horse training techniques.

Training horses requires guidance and a willingness to listen to the pupil's reaction. With this understanding, Jack points out that in training, we, as amateurs or professionals, are dealing with thinking beings. These thinking animals will react to our instructions, our cues, and our exercises, and we in turn must develop our willingness to listen, and our awareness of the way they think.

Western Training: Theory & Practice is designed to be a guide and an approach to help people think through their horse training programs. On one level it is a basic training book; on another level it attempts to say: Be innovative. Think how your horse is responding and design *your* program to suit your horse.

Perhaps, as I analyze Jack Brainard's theories and his practices, we are returned to the basics of light horse ownership. We are reminded indirectly that we are engaged in a communicative process—a process of building a working friendship/relationship. As horse trainers we are seeking to be guides and friends, and, as such, to provide support systems for our horses, remembering that each horse needs different kinds of support. I think Jack Brainard has made a strong contribution to the body of knowledge available to trainers of horses. I have been pleased to be a part of it.
                                    —Peter Phinny

CONTENTS

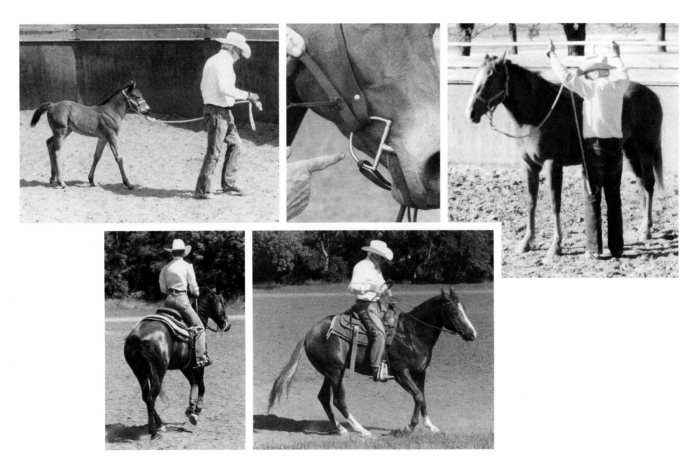

1 HALTER-BREAKING:
INTRODUCING A THEORY

This chapter serves more to illustrate my approach to training rather than to give specific instruction.

Western Training: Theory and Practice is intended to complement those books dealing with particular topics such as horse breaking and stable management, as well as those focusing on specialized training such as reining, cutting, barrel racing, etc. What I hope that this book will do is provide riders with a way to think about training and to solve training problems.

I hope that it will encourage trainers to recognize a soft, quiet approach; an approach that will cause their horses the least anxiety and produce the least resistance. This book is not merely a series of exercises, techniques, or suggested ma-

neuvers. If I'm successful, it will give trainers, riders, owners, and handlers a way to figure out how to get ideas across to a horse, to offer the horse ideas in a manner that does not cause him fear, and in a manner that provides the horseman the chance to understand the horse's reaction to those ideas.

In this spirit, this chapter dealing with halter-breaking is included not specifically for purposes of instruction and technique, but rather as an example of the approach to training, which is the fundamental core of this book.

As you no doubt already know, the true horseman continually looks for

Normally I halter-break my colts after they are weaned, but since we took the photographs for this chapter in the spring, we used a 2-week-old filly. While we secure the halter and lead rope, mother inspects us.

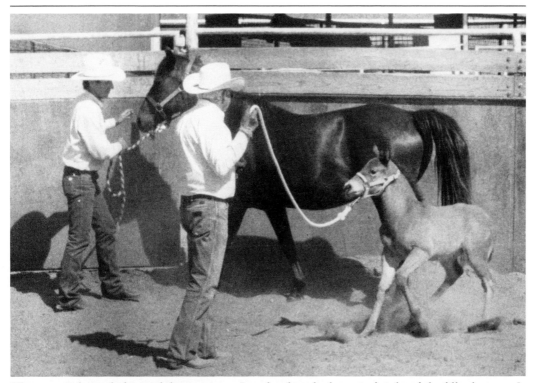

The mare is being led out of the pen now. I prefer that she be out of sight of the filly, because I feel I will gain the filly's attention more quickly, and she will retain the lesson better than if the mare was present. I want to give the filly the chance to think through the process I'm going to introduce to her. (Note: If the mare gets terribly upset at being separated from her foal, it would be wiser to leave her in the pen, with someone holding her. Generally, the younger the foal, the more distraught the mare will be at even a brief separation.)

better ways to communicate with his horse, and he understands that communication requires listening, "listening" to his horse. I am constantly advising horsemen to watch their horses. I don't think that trainers can be reminded enough times to let their horses "tell" them their reactions. Observe your horse at all times, and try to think like him.

Foals can be halter-broke at any age, and there are advantages and disadvantages in doing it before they are weaned, or waiting until after they are weaned. A very young foal that hasn't been weaned is easier to handle because he is smaller, but his attention span is only about a minute long, and he will probably be distracted by his mother. A weaned colt, on the other hand, has a longer attention span, but he is larger, stronger, and might be more difficult to handle.

I personally prefer to halter-break my colts after they are weaned, and this chapter is written from that viewpoint. However, we took the photographs for this chapter in the spring and had to use a young foal. This filly was about two weeks old. My approach to halter-

breaking is basically the same, regardless of the youngster's age. Remember: We are most interested in suggesting a way to think about training and communicating with horses that can be used in all phases of training on horses of all ages.

I also want to mention that although I use the collective term *colts* throughout this book, the information, of course, also applies to fillies.

After the colt has been weaned from his dam, and when he has gained enough self-confidence so that his thoughts are not totally consumed with the absence of his mother, and when he'll give you his attention rather than exhibit fear, it is time to begin.

You need to gently earn your colt's acceptance and then his trust. Take your time, pet him, and gently through the course of several sessions ease on a weanling-size halter with an attached lead rope (not a leather strap or chain). It is best to have the weanling in a rather small area to begin with. A box stall is fine. Later you can take him out of the stall, but initially even the restraint of a halter can be a very spooky prospect for a youngster, no matter

The filly is upset and, of course, doesn't understand what I want. So I'm not fighting her. I'm moving with her as she backs up—staying toward her head and not letting her turn her hindquarters to me. I'm taking my time, allowing her to think through the halter-breaking process, rather than forcing it on her.

how docile he seems.

Over the centuries horses have developed their physical senses in order to survive. Flight, or fleeing from danger, is a characteristic of the horse with which all horsemen are familiar. This is one of nature's contributions. Coupled with this instinct to run from danger is the means to detect danger. A horse's vision is a fundamental sense used in the detection of possible danger, and vision is directly linked to the positioning of the head. Horses simply do not see in the same way that humans do.

As an example, when a horse pricks his ears and holds his head up, his vision is focused on something in the distance. He must position his head in order to

You need to gently earn your colt's acceptance and then his trust.

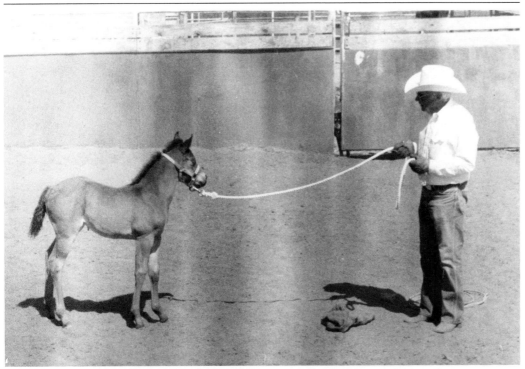

The filly has stopped going backwards, and I'm talking to her, allowing her to relax. I need her attention, and she must be allowed her own composure and calmness to have a chance to think.

If she's not calm and if I don't have her quiet attention, I can't teach her anything. Remember, I'm working with her mind, not her body; I'm trying to communicate with her. Obviously, her attention is not on me yet. But if I were to jerk her around, she'd become tense and would definitely not be in a frame of mind to think about learning to lead. I'm just keeping a pound or two of pressure on the lead rope and am waiting for her.

Now the filly is beginning to pay a bit more attention to me. In the beginning, it will be easier for her to step to the side, rather than straight forward, so I'm standing to the side of her. I've drawn the slack out of the lead and am applying maybe two pounds of pressure, and am just standing calmly and waiting.

focus his vision; he cannot simply focus his eyes as a human might.

Incidentally, in this posture with his focus in the distance, he cannot see the one to four feet of ground lying directly in front of himself. Given this example, it follows that if one puts a halter on a colt and jerks him around, restricting his head position, one has restricted his ability to focus his eyes properly. This might be frightening for any of God's creatures, let alone a freshly weaned colt.

So how do we approach the colt? Do we pull him around until he's afraid to do anything other than follow us? Put a rope around his hindquarters and force him to step forward? When using these approaches, the chances are that with considerable effort and quite a bit of dust stirring, eventually we could convince a weanling to walk forward on a lead rope.

The chances are equally good that in a couple of quiet sessions we can have the colt following on a slack lead rope if we're willing to put him in a non-restrained position and allow him to think for himself, to search for the slack in the lead.

"But," some horsemen say, "I don't want a kid-broke horse. I don't want a horse I have to pet into everything.

That's a spoiled horse." These are natural reactions; I've heard this kind of response and at one time would have reacted this way myself. I am not suggesting that you spoil a colt, in the same way that you'd be remiss if you spoiled your son or daughter.

What I am proposing is that you allow your weanling to think, that you set up a situation which allows him to decide to move forward when you ask him to. If this action is his idea, the chances are very good that he'll remember the sessions as pleasant, and that he'll feel good about the accomplishment rather than remember the fear of being pulled around without understanding the purpose of it all.

"All right," the skeptics say, "so how do you halter-break a colt without pulling on him, tying him to a burro, or putting a rope around his hindquarters?"

Well, with your colt in a halter with a long lead rope, allow him to back into a corner of the stall, or against a wall of the pen, or to the end of the lead rope—whatever he wants to do. Try not to fight him, but do try to keep towards his head rather than his hindquarters. (You'll probably have to start in a stall, but as soon as he's ready, move to a little larger area. A round pen is ideal.)

The pressure is simply something for her to think about and figure out. I'm not forcing her. As soon as she so much as leans toward me, I give her slack. I'm showing her that she can lean, step, or walk toward the pressure and find relief, as she's doing here.

He'll very likely try to avoid you, to get away from you, and he'll probably turn his left side toward you or perhaps his hindquarters towards you. He may fight a bit; he may rear up and show his confusion. His hindquarters are his defensive weapons and even a weanling can deliver painful kicks, so be careful.

You should be able to calmly avoid being caught in a corner. Try not to pressure him or think you need to "make" him do something. When he tries to evade and to pull away, the secret is to hold him firmly so that when he pulls on you, you don't pull or jerk on him.

Watch him, talk to him, and allow him to relax as much as he can. You need his attention and he must be allowed his own composure and calmness in order to have a chance to think. If he's not calm and if you do not have his quiet attention, you won't be able to teach him anything. You are working with his mind, not his body. Remember this because in every training session you have with a horse, you will be working with his mind trying to communicate with him. If you can get your idea across to your pupil, his body will take care of itself—it will do the best that it is capable of doing at that particular time.

Stand off to one side of your colt, not directly in front of him. Now draw any slack out of the lead. Just draw out the slack and apply maybe one or two

Reward your foal after he moves, even if it is barely noticeable. At first, putting slack in the rope is reward enough. Eventually, he'll probably let you gently rub him, as the filly has. Rewarding a foal builds his confidence.

Now I'm working in a semicircular pattern on both the left and right sides of the filly, before asking her to step straight toward me. Here, she has taken a step to the side, and I've rewarded her with slack.

It's obvious here that the little filly is thinking a lot more than she was, and that I also have her attention. What I'm doing is asking her to take a step toward me.

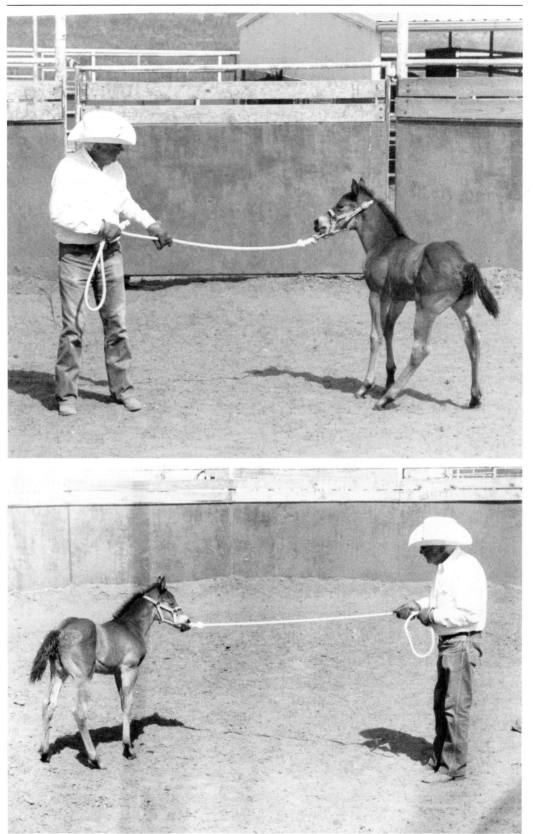

14

She's taken a step toward me, and I've immediately given her slack.

pounds of pressure. Stand calmly and wait. Be patient, and don't pull on the colt. A horse can feel a fly on his skin, so he's sensitive enough to feel the slight one pound of pressure on the lead rope. Eventually he will move in order to relieve the annoyance of the very slight pressure.

If you pull forward with too much pressure, or if you jerk him, his natural reaction will be to pull back. He'll try to get away from you. This one pound of pressure is not enough to scare the colt, to cause him to seek flight, back up, or rear. The pressure is simply something for him to think about and to figure out. Just wait for him, and watch him carefully. You are setting up the situation for him, not forcing him to do something.

When he so much as *leans* toward you

to remove the pressure, give him slack. Show him that he can lean, step, or walk towards the pressure and find relief. Reward him after he moves, even if it is barely noticeable. Watch him and wait for him to shift his weight in the correct direction, to step forward—however he moves in order to find the slack in the rope. Then praise him and try to gently stroke him if he'll let you.

Wait a minute and then once again draw the slack out of your lead rope. Be patient. It may take your colt five minutes to figure this thing out. He'll probably work his ears, he may back into a corner, but all the while he'll be thinking and all you do is keep the slight pressure on. Remember this amount of pressure is only a taut lead, it isn't even a tug. Keep repeating the process. If he does start

15

Anyone can force a horse to perform exercises, but to become an accomplished trainer and horseman, one needs to be a student of the horse.

In just a few minutes, the filly happily walks forward, keeping slack in the rope. She's telling me that she trusts me, and is ready to be led wherever I want to go. She has confidence, and I've done nothing to jeopardize our future relationship with her. And she will remember this lesson well because she was allowed to think and figure it out for herself.

backing up, don't fight him; simply go with him, keeping the same amount of light pressure on the rope.

You are asking him to create slack in the rope. Work around him in semicircular positions, waiting each time for him to understand, and to take a step or two towards you. Work in a semicircular pattern on both his right and left sides before asking him to take a step directly forward, straight towards you. Stepping directly forward is a big accomplishment; in the beginning, it's easier for him to step towards the side rather than forward.

Before long you'll probably be able to communicate the concept, and your colt will understand what you want him to do. He'll remember it because you allowed him to figure it out. You also won't run the risk of creating an atmosphere of apprehension and fear in your colt, and he'll be that much more willing

to try whatever you have in store for him next time.

Of course, colts have been trained to lead in many different ways throughout centuries. What is important, and the reason this example is included in a book on western training theory and practice, is that continually cultivating an ability to think and communicate with your horse, to be aware of what he is trying to tell you, and to see his fears and concerns, is the key to effective training. Anyone can force a horse to perform exercises, but to become an accomplished trainer and horseman, one needs to be a student of the horse. Like a first-grader, a horse will try to get along if the teacher is considerate enough to explain what needs to be done. If you scare your colt or try to get him to lead, he'll think about what scares him, not about what relieves his anxiety.

It takes no talent to hook and spur a

Horses do not see in the same way that humans do. A horse must position his head in order to focus his vision; he cannot simply focus his eyes as a human might. Although I'd like this colt's attention to be on me, he's obviously seen something in the distance. It's important to know where your horse's attention is focused so that you do not force him to do something he is not prepared to do, and end up scaring or fighting him. **Photo by Peter Phinny**

horse into performing an adequate maneuver. It takes a real horseman to develop and guide a horse. In this book I hope to offer some of the theory and practice I have learned, not just so that I can solve particular problems, but rather so that I can offer a way for each individual to think and to approach his training goals and problems. I want each of us, myself included, to remember the importance of concentrating on our horse's mind, and to be able to set up situations so that our horse is allowed to think his way into the execution of a maneuver.

Now, before we begin chapter two, I have something that I want you to keep in mind while reading this book. Training should be a challenge for both the horse and for the rider, and it should be enjoyable. So, understand the ideas, the approach, and the principles that the following chapters try to cover, but don't get bogged down. Continually work to develop greater and easier ways to communicate the task you want your horse to perform. And above all, have respect for your horse.

2 CARE AND MANAGEMENT
THE FIRST TWO YEARS

A horse needs about 2 percent of his body weight daily in a combination of hay and grain to maintain his weight.

There are many theories on the care and management of horses, and nearly all horse-oriented people are well-educated in this area. As a matter of fact, when we have met our horse's nutritional needs and have given him plenty of exercise, we have just about satisfied his basic requirements. In most cases, the colt's management hinges on the owner's facilities, and the facilities will dictate how the colt is cared for. If the colt's owner has a small place with few horses, the colt will most likely spend his yearling year close to the barn. In this environment he will be subject to more care, more handling, and more association with humans than a ranch-raised colt. The atmosphere will make him a different colt than the one who spends his first year in a large pasture with other colts and receives little or no attention.

Personally, I feel that the colt that runs in pasture with other horses will develop into a better horse. This colt has learned to compete with other horses and to cope with the pecking order. When he is handled later in his life, he will be more attentive, show his trainer more respect, and in general be a better pupil. We're discussing preferences here, so don't rush out and sell your colt if he's been raised close to the barn because, above all, a quality colt will make a good horse whether he spent his yearling year on the range or in the paddock.

Feed is important and it should be adequate in order to ensure proper growth. The main point to remember is to give him enough. All feed companies have excellent programs for raising colts and developing sound, healthy year-lings. Grain is important for a colt's growth. Most horsemen seem to feel that they are authorities on equine nutrition and almost all have a favorite ration or program. A horse needs about 2 percent of his body weight daily in a combination of grain and hay to maintain his weight; not to gain weight, only to maintain it. Within this quantity it is important that the colt's ration contain an adequate protein level, along with the proper calcium/phosphorous balance.

Be cautious about feeding too much grain, however, as that can cause contracted tendons and epiphysitis, and other bone damage in weanlings and yearlings. As a rule of thumb, feed 1/2 pound of grain per 100 pounds of body weight.

Vitamins are important, and a vitamin program will depend on the condition of the pasture in which the colt runs. A lush pasture may adequately supply a colt's vitamin needs; some grain rations contain adequate vitamin requirements, provided the colt gets a sufficient amount. If you need advice, don't be afraid to seek out an expert. Perhaps you can contact your county agricultural agent, the animal science department at your state university, your veterinarian, or even a feed company.

On the subject of hay, there is a tremendous variance. The protein level of two hay samples which may look similar can differ by 10-12 percentage points. If you aren't pretty savvy on the subject of hay, find someone who is.

I am reminded of the story told by a friend of mine about the hay buyer who

Personally, I feel that the colt that runs in pasture with other horses will develop into a better horse. This colt has to learn to compete with other horses and to cope with the pecking order. Later, when he is being handled, he will show his trainer more respect, will be more attentive, and in general be a better pupil.

asked the farmer what he wanted for his hay. The farmer asked $3 a bale, at which the buyer replied, "That's too much. I can buy your neighbor's hay for half of that." The farmer said, "Well, if you want hen nests and dog beds, buy his hay, but if you want feed, then that's a different matter."

Truer words about hay were never spoken. There can be a heck of a difference in the quality of one hay versus another. Run a check on the protein content and the percentage of TDN (total digestible nutrients) before you lay in a winter's supply.

The next item of major importance is a worming program. This is so important and most of us are lax in this area. It is almost a certainty that most yearlings are infested since none are raised on sterile ground anymore. With today's paste wormers, however, it is easy to keep parasites under control. It is best to change brands periodically to keep a colt from developing an immunity to a particular formula, and it is important to worm on a regular schedule. Once or

twice a year is not enough. You can obtain advice as well as worming products from your vet.

If your colt was halter-broke as a weanling, you are in good shape. If not, halter-break him as soon as possible. Teach him to lead properly as we discussed in chapter one. If you have to drag him around, he is not halter-broke. Make sure also that your halter fits him, but never leave a halter on him when he's loose in pasture, a corral, or even in a stall. It is the mark of an amateur. Each year many horses are killed or crippled because careless owners leave halters on them, and the halters hang up on something.

19

Make sure your halter fits correctly; but never leave the halter on your horse when he is loose in his stall, pasture, corral—anywhere. Each year many horses are killed or crippled because careless owners turned them loose with a halter on.

Opinions vary on how much we can ask of a colt at a young age. While many colts are started at 18 to 20 months of age, I'll wait a little longer with mine. I think their mental attitude will improve with a few extra months. **Photo by Peter Phinny**

Feet need periodic attention. A yearling's feet are important and a good farrier can do lots to shape his feet for the rest of his life. Corrective measures taken during the yearling year will have more effect than at any time thereafter. It is always best to trim a colt at natural angles, angles that are the same angle formed by his pasterns.

A competent farrier can work wonders with a yearling's feet. Depending on conditions underfoot, a colt's feet probably should be trimmed every three months and more often if needed. A colt running on dry, hard, or rocky ground will need less trimming than one in a soft, grassy pasture. The amount of wear on the foot depends entirely on the footing. If a colt's feet were trimmed when he was halter-broke, trimming will be that much easier when he's a bit older. Even if a colt's feet have not been trimmed, they should at least be handled and picked up before the farrier arrives.

The topic of how much training we give our yearlings is controversial. Conditions determine this; if your time isn't a factor, and if the colt is available (not out in a pasture), we can probably teach him lots of things: standing quietly to be groomed, exercising on a longe line, how to load quietly in a trailer, how to stand to be saddled, and much more.

With intense training programs, opinions vary as to how much we can ask of a yearling. Big, early colts properly grown out and raised under barnyard conditions are sometimes ready to be saddled during the fall of their yearling year. We see many of them started at 18 to 20 months of age. The 2-year-old pleasure futurities definitely have a bearing on this. If a colt is mature for his age, if his knees are closed, and if he is limited to short rides with no stress (no rollbacks, hard stops, etc.), this might be okay.

Personally, I'll wait a little longer with mine. I think their mental attitude will improve with a few extra months. Remember, they are only babies; give them all the breaks that you can. Let them grow up and have the time they need to make nice horses. If you watch them, they'll tell you when they're ready. And almost any veterinarian will tell you that the longer you wait to start riding a young horse, the fewer soundness problems he will have later on.

In most cases, the colt's management hinges on the owner's facilities. If his owner has a small place, the colt will most likely spend his yearling year close to the barn.

Hay and grain are important and an adequate amount should be fed to ensure growth. However, an excessive amount of grain can cause epiphysitis and other problems. Although the colts shown here spend their time exclusively in pasture, they are grained daily.

Photos by Peter Phinny

21

3 SELECTING A PROSPECT

Pedigree, disposition, conformation, structure of the legs and feet, mental attitude and willingness, and coordination should all be considered.

In my opinion, bloodlines in any breed will tell us a lot about a young horse's potential, and to ignore it is being very shortsighted. In Quarter Horse pedigrees, I feel that King P-234 has been the most dominant sire in the breed's history. Personally, I'll pay little attention to a horse or a pedigree if there isn't quite a concentration of King showing up.

"I knew the minute I saw him that he was a winner." How many times have we heard this statement. Everyone has his or her ideas on the selection of a horse, and particularly on the selection of a performance prospect.

Since my childhood, I have run into many old-timers (and many young horsemen as well) who feel that they can look at a young horse's conformation, watch him move, and then accurately decide as to his performance potential. What they are saying, in effect, is that they could go to the Keeneland Thoroughbred Yearling Sale and, without benefit of the catalog, select a Derby winner.

It can't be done no matter how much we'd like to perpetuate the romance of the "horseman's eye" approach to buying horses. There are simply so many factors involved that to intelligently select a winner, consideration must be given to all of them. Even after giving the proper weight to all of the factors, the results often go awry. Nevertheless, during this process of

Here is a nice group of 2-year-olds. Seeing prospects together helps one compare disposition, conformation, and athletic ability. Of course, you never really know enough until the actual riding and training stage, but we must learn as much as possible in order to intelligently pick our prospects.

selection we are trying to work the odds in our favor, and even then a longshot can upset us. In my estimation the following factors, details, and/or situations deserve consideration: pedigree, disposition, conformation, structure of the legs and feet, mental attitude and willingness, and coordination. I am probably leaving out other elements, but if one pays attention to these, the chances for success will be good.

Pedigree. In my opinion, blood will tell a lot and to fail to consider it is very shortsighted. Breeders have selected outstanding stallions to breed to outstanding mares for generations and with a good deal of success. It is foolish not to consider the pedigree. I am most familiar with Quarter Horses, but the principle applies to all breeds.

In most cases, successful breeders breed for specific purposes, and it is therefore easier for us to select our horses if we study the pedigrees and select from horse families strong in the events or activities that hold our inter-est. It would be wise to enlist the help of someone well-versed in pedigrees if you doubt the veracity or quality of a particular pedigree.

Most geneticists feel that the first two or three generations are the important horses to consider, and that the horses farther back in the pedigree are insignificant. I want mine to evidence quality all the way back, and quality to me means solid production records and/or performance records.

Using Quarter Horse pedigrees as a case in point, I feel that King P-234 has been the most dominant sire in the breed's history. Personally, I pay little attention to a horse or to a pedigree if there isn't quite a concentration of King showing up. The more the better. There is no way to disregard King if one is looking for a trainable Quarter Horse.

With today's computer magic it is easy to research any horse's pedigree. Breed associations' print-outs give us show records and performance records of any registered horse, as well as all the

23

Often when young horses are turned loose together, they give us an indication of their temperaments. Sometimes a colt or filly who is bossy and "rules the roost" (such as the colt on the far left) will bear a little watching; he might not be too eager to respond to a handler or rider.

dominant horses in his pedigree. Mares and stallions can be checked for their produce records. In fact, we can determine with amazing accuracy the background of any horse that might interest us. This tool is invaluable in helping us with a pedigree.

I'm an advocate of the record-keeping done by the breed associations—we need to make more use of this storehouse of information. Whatever events or activities interest you, find out whether a prospective horse's ancestors were accomplished in this area or whether they produced successful horses. Don't hesitate to ask: "How is he bred?"

Disposition. I know of no factor in the process of training a horse that is as important as disposition. What is disposition? Webster defines it as "one's temperament" and temperament, Webster says, is "one's frame of mind." This is the heart of the subject of disposition. I know that if I can keep a fresh and positive frame of mind in my pupil, that training is much

easier and the results will be faster than if he resists what I'm asking him to try. With a good frame of mind, training begins to be fun for both of us.

A horse with a nice disposition is so evident. He puts up with a trainer's mistakes. He quietly allows himself to be put into strange and uncomfortable situations. He doesn't tense up and try to prance, dance, or charge off all over the training area. A colt with a good disposition is forgiving when we issue the wrong cues or unjustifiably reprimand him. It's about that simple. Even an amateur horseman recognizes a good, kind disposition, because without it, all trainers are in trouble.

I feel that disposition is definitely inherited. Horses have a good disposition or they don't, and we can't train it into them if they don't. An excerpt from an old Austrian cavalry manual expresses my feeling pretty well: "Defects of disposition are harder to correct than defects of conformation."

Dispositions—good and bad—manifest themselves at an early age. Even weanlings will give us an idea about their dispositions if we study them. By the time they are yearlings or twos, it's easy to read them.

Beginners in the training process are wiped out if their horses don't manifest good dispositions. I can't think of anything that turns me off more than to try to train an unwilling, sour horse. It's mostly wasted effort. We can locate horses with similar conformation, age, breeding, etc., but if these horses have different frames of mind, the results will be phenomenally different.

A good disposition manifests itself at an early age. Weanlings give an idea about their dispositions particularly when halter-breaking them. The ones with the good dispositions are friendly and inquisitive. They love to be rubbed and petted. I'll take the ones with this attitude every time.

Sometimes when colts are turned loose in a pen together, they indicate their temperaments. Often a colt who is bossy and rules the roost, so to speak, will bear a little watching; he might not be too eager to respond to us. A loner may evidence a tendency to be incompatible or, on the other side of the coin, smart enough to feel his way out of trouble. Constantly watching and studying the colts will tell us lots about them; invariably they will, at some juncture, "betray their hand" and tell us what they are really like.

Conformation. I think every horseman feels that he or she is somewhat of an authority on conformation and has no difficulty deciding on what he or she likes and dislikes, nor about what's wrong with the neighbor's horse. I think, however, that we can go overboard worrying about minute details of conformation. Probably from a trainer's standpoint, conformation isn't all that important. We see lots of great horses in the winner's circle that are by no means beautifully conformed by halter-horse standards. We can all cite cases in point; we see horses doing hard jobs and doing them well that, by arbitrary standards, do not have the proper conformation for the job.

This young horse has the kind, gentle eye I like to see in a performance prospect.

To turn an otherwise great horse down because of a minor conformation defect is insane.

This is not to say that there are not some basic elements of structure of which we must be aware. A few points do bear watching. Clean-necked horses do bridle (flex) more easily than thick, cumbersome-necked horses. Horses with sloping shoulders hit the ground more softly than straight-shouldered horses. High-withered horses carry the saddle better than mutton-withered horses, and heavily loined horses stop better than horses with weak muscling in their loins.

Low-necked horses seem to be a little easier to turn around than high, goose-necked horses. A little set, a slight angle, in a horse's hocks doesn't hurt his stop, but too much set paves the way for an injury such as a curb. Most horsemen also like a long hip and croup.

The size of a horse is important to many, but not to me. In my view a little horse can outdo a big one every time. They turn around better and faster, roll back more powerfully, respond better, and stop harder than their taller counterparts.

I am constantly aware of people who are size nuts, especially the Europeans, who think it is a disgrace to ride anything smaller than a 16-hand horse when, in my estimation, a 14.2 horse could probably do the job better. I can name dozens of horses under 14.3 that

were the world's greatest. The best 16-hand horse going couldn't have started to perform with them. If I were riding across a 50-mile pasture, I think size might help, but there aren't many 50-mile pastures anymore.

To turn an otherwise great horse down because of a minor conformation defect is insane. Conformation in a performance horse is overplayed. Give me a nice-minded, coordinated athlete, and I'll worry about size and conformation later.

Legs and Feet. We can't downplay underpinning in a performance horse since our biggest challenge during the training process may be to keep him sound. This problem in the Thoroughbred business is highly significant, and fortunes have been lost because of the unsoundnesses in speed horses. A horse in motion exerts tremendous pressure on muscles, tendons, ligaments, and feet.

The structure of the feet and legs have an absolute bearing on soundness. Most equine vets are thoroughly familiar with leg problems and are pretty knowledgeable as to causes of lamenesses, particularly if they are related to the structure of the foot and leg. Once diagnosed, a leg problem can be researched by any horseman, since volumes of information are available.

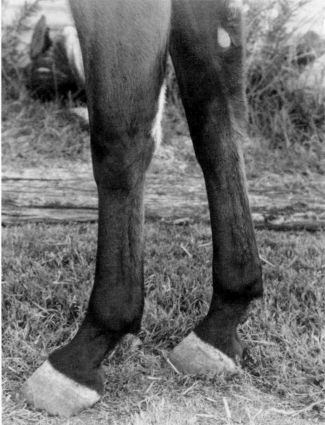

These front legs show good, sound structure, with short cannon bones.

Here's a young horse who has correct front leg alignment.

I cannot downplay structure because structural soundness is important even in horses without exemplary conformation. We are not looking for halter-horse conformation, but good bone and body structure that is aligned, one part with the next, so that undue pressure is not exerted on a weakness. This 2-year-old filly has straight hind legs with sound structure.

Photo by Peter Phinny

This 2-year-old filly was pasture-raised prior to being started under saddle. She has an alert but composed attitude; she's a little wary, but not wild-eyed or goofy. She has good conformation and would definitely warrant consideration as a performance-horse prospect.

Photo by Peter Phinny

I have obviously made a distinction between conformation, as discussed in the previous entry, and structure. I have downplayed conformation because of the excellent performers that have less-than-perfect halter-class conformation. I cannot downplay structure because structural soundness is important even in horses without exemplary conformation.

From a structural standpoint, certain types of injuries are prone to appear on certain types of conformation below the knees and hocks. One is likely, for instance, to "pop" a curb on a horse that is sickle-hocked—a horse with an exaggerated set to his hocks. Curbs are common on hard-stopping horses even if they have excellent structure, because there is a tremendous amount of pressure exerted on the tendons and ligaments when a horse stops hard. A sickle-hocked horse is just that much more prone to developing this problem.

A short- or straight-pasterned horse does not have much natural shock-absorbing, and this trait may result in bone disorders, especially at the articulation of the joints. Such disorders can be manifested in anything from a jack or spavin to a ringbone. A horse's gait can also contribute to soundness problems. Standardbred trainers are familiar with this. They constantly have problems

28

A horse in motion exerts tremendous pressure on muscles, tendons, ligaments, bones, and feet. This is why one should be cautious about putting too much stress on 2-year-olds. Notice the amount of pressure exerted on the right front and the left hind of this horse.

Photo by Peter Phinny

with forging, interfering, brushing, clipping, knee-knocking, and others.

During the training process, many times a horse will sore up. Trainers should pay attention to any indication of soreness because the horse is telling us that he has a problem and that something needs to be done before it reappears in a much more acute form. Treatment might require rest, medication, or additional farrier work. The important thing when a problem appears is not to overlook it, or to take a wait-and-see attitude.

It is also important to remember that many foot and leg problems can be avoided if the horse is properly conditioned and brought gradually into the stressful part of the training. I want to emphasize this; conditioning is very important. Doctors who treat pro athletes tell us that most injuries occur when athletes are tired or tiring. A large number of all football injuries happen in the fourth quarter. Thoroughbred trainers tell us that most of the race-related injuries occur during the last quarter-mile of the race. Here again we can learn something: Don't ask a horse for hard maneuvers when he is tired. Watch him; he'll tell you.

Mental Attitude and Willingness. Everything works best when our own MA is on target, and the same thing applies for the horse. If we can create or channel the proper frame of mind in our trainee, we can expect positive results and efforts. To achieve a good and positive learning attitude in a horse, a trainer must constantly try to keep his horse in situations where he is not stressed, uncomfortable, afraid, mad, or agitated.

At almost every stage and training level, the horse's mental attitude and willingness to learn are perhaps the most crucial factors affecting long-term success. Throughout the chapters of this book we will approach these two

29

Here's a 3-year-old colt with a nice relaxed, content attitude, and who is really listening to Kim Diercks. A good mental attitude is so important to the effectiveness of a training program.

A horse with a nice disposition puts up with trainer's mistakes. He quietly allows himself to be put into strange and uncomfortable situations. He doesn't tense up and try to charge or prance. This 3-year-old stud colt is out of position, but he's trying and he has a nice attitude.

elements over and over again. For the most part, when training a horse, I am convinced that we must deal with the horse's mind first, and that the physical maneuver desired at any particular juncture will take care of itself. This doesn't mean that if you are a good communicator and developer of your horse's mental attitude, you will end up with the O.J. Simpson of the horse world. What it does mean is that you can expect your horse to perform to the best of his nature-given abilities.

If we have selected a horse that demonstrates willingness and a calm, positive mental attitude when challenged, and if we are able to maintain and foster this, then we are on our way to making a nice horse. It is unbelievable how much we can teach our colt if his MA is right.

Coordination. Many horses exhibit all the positive indications that they will be top performance horses. Sometimes, however, the simple matter of coordination becomes a factor. A coordinated horse does everything easily; he executes hard maneuvers easily. He is graceful, his movements are fluid, and he positions himself quickly. Beware of the horse who constantly misses his leads and then makes no attempt to correct himself. Leads are a dead giveaway, and coordinated horses rarely miss them.

A trainer will soon realize the level of coordination possessed by his horse. If a horse is slow or hesitant about stepping with his inside foot in the direction of the pull, he might not be too well coordinated. If it is difficult for him to back up, and if he is dragging his feet rather than lifting them backwards, this might indicate a lack of coordination.

The point here is to recognize the coordinated individual, and the varying levels of coordination, and to approach this horse with good judgment and patience. However coordinated your horse, you can help him to become a well-schooled individual. Trouble will result, nevertheless, if you ask a horse to perform beyond his innate ability, in the same way that asking a 6'7" basketball player to play hockey could produce a frustrated athlete.

Many people prefer big horses, but not me. In my view, little horses can outperform big ones almost every time. They can turn around better and faster, roll-back more powerfully, respond better, and stop harder than their taller counterparts. A superb example was Lynx Melody, winner of the 1978 National Cutting Horse Association Futurity, who stood only 13.2 hands. She was ridden by Larry Reeder, and owned by Billy Cogdell, Tulia, Texas.

Photo Courtesy of NCHA

To conclude this chapter regarding the selection of a horse, my advice is to watch a prospective purchase or trainee carefully and use good, common-sense judgment. Know what you want to do with your horse and try to approach a prospect's strengths and weaknesses as they apply to your program, given the basic traits that we have discussed. In regard to the physical characteristics of any prospect, don't hesitate to do some research on structure, or to enlist the help of an expert. Paying for a physical examination is a lot cheaper than buying a problem.

Coordination is a major key to becoming a top performance horse. A coordinated horse does everything easily, including hard maneuvers. He is graceful, his movements are fluid, and he positions himself quickly.

Photo by Peter Phinny

4 FIRST SADDLING

Photo by Peter Phinny

This chapter provides a transition from handling and preparing a colt to that moment when one actually swings a leg over him.

There have been many methods and programs devised by man to begin the actual process of training a horse to carry a rider. Volumes can be written on the basic stages of training, and there are good books currently available on this subject. I would advise trainers, both professionals and non-professionals, to read whatever is available and to constantly search for better ways and varying techniques to train your horses.

For the purpose of this book, we will approach the first saddling of the green colt in a brief and somewhat philosophical manner. We are, after all, most concerned with the colt's behavior and with his mental reaction to our suggestions.

This chapter, brief as it is, provides a transition from handling and preparing a colt, to that moment when one actually swings a leg over him and attempts to communicate from his back. As such, it is as much a theoretical introduction to our program as it is a method for

The Diamond B Ranch is strictly a working outfit; the only real difference between our show equipment and our everyday training equipment is the polish and saddle soap used to clean it up. Here's a view of one wall of the shop/tack room.

Photo by Peter Phinny

the first saddling.

I should note at this point that I've made several assumptions regarding the readers' level of understanding. I have taken for granted some knowledge of tack, parts of the horse, and basic horsemanship. These topics are for the most part commonplace and covered in the work of other writers. Devoting substantial print to them would limit the space available to us for the subject matter of this book.

Another assumption is that any reader of a book like this is a student of the horse; throughout this book there may be terms and concepts that a diligent reader will need to look up or further research. This is the nature of the process of learning anything from mathematics to racquetball.

On the very specific topic of bits (and of bitting the horse), I would like to

This full-cheek snaffle is one example of a true snaffle bit. It has no shanks and, therefore, no leverage action. This bit, like all true snaffles, works from a direct rein.

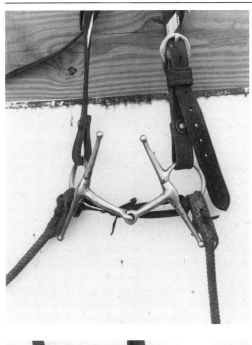

clarify an often misused notion. A true snaffle bit, which we will refer to throughout this book, has no curb strap, shank, or leverage action, and works from a direct or snaffle rein. There are many varieties of snaffle bits such as D-rings, O-rings, egg-butts, and full-cheeks; and the most widely used snaffles have a broken mouthpiece, which is easy on a horse's mouth.

Any bit relying on leverage action and which requires using a curb strap or chain is a curb bit, regardless of whether or not the mouthpiece is broken or solid. A curb bit requires a horse to understand the use of the indirect rein which, in western training, is the neck rein. Curb bits are used on horses that have finished, or are in the process of finishing, their training. A grazing bit is a common

Here are four examples of a curb bit. Top left is a Pelham, which I like to use when making the transition from the snaffle to a curb bit. It allows for both snaffle and curb reins to be used. Top right: a curb with a hinged mouthpiece, made by Ray Maheu. Bottom left: a Greg Darnall curb bit with swivel shanks and rings for snaffle reins. Bottom right: a Buster Welch, a useful and popular design that horses seem to accept comfortably.

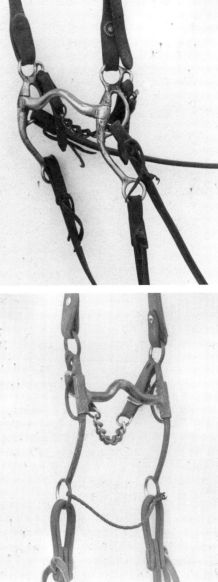

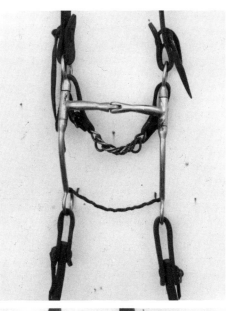

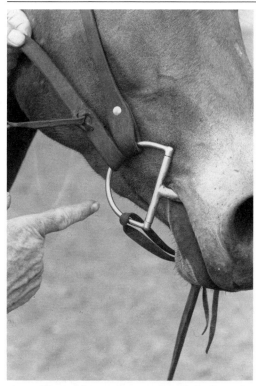

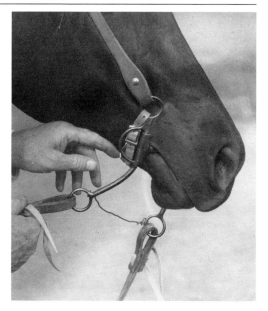

The shanks of the curb bit working together with the curb strap (or chain) put leverage action on the bars of the mouth. This is a radically different sensation than that of a snaffle bit, and that's why a colt must be eased into a curb gradually. Because of the way the curb bit works, it is best used with an indirect (neck) rein when turning the horse.

A snaffle works on the corners of the horse's mouth and allows the rider to position the horse's body through direct reining.

example of a curb bit; so is a Tom Thumb bit, which is often mistakenly called a snaffle.

The broken mouthpiece of a snaffle should also be large enough in diameter so as to not cut the corners of a horse's mouth.

I am a firm believer in snaffle-bit training and in taking the time necessary to teach the horse to perform proficiently in the snaffle. Only when the horse is calm and comfortable with the various maneuvers should he be moved out of the snaffle.

As a transitional bit, I like to use a Pelham and double reins. This is my preference and this becomes evident a little farther into this book. Nevertheless, in making the transition from the direct snaffle rein to the curb bit and indirect rein, many trainers choose bosals, broken-mouthpiece curb bits, and various combinations of bosals, snaffles, and curbs.

The point here is to achieve adequate or proper communication with your horse. A curb bit with a curb strap puts lever-action pressure on the bars of the mouth. A snaffle works on the corners of the mouth and best allows for direct-rein positioning of the horse's body.

I use a Pelham after a colt becomes supple and proficient in a snaffle—in order to introduce him to the feel of the curb bit and indirect rein with as little confusion as possible.

These are radically different sensations for your horse and as such must be communicated gradually.

As is the case at every stage of training, we must wait for the horse to indicate to us that he is ready to move to a more advanced bit. Neck-reining (the indirect rein), used as a cue on the horse's neck, can be easily accomplished if it is introduced so that the horse understands the pressure and the sensation.

In regard to the bits used on horses in the various photographs, they should not be considered "the" bit to use for the particular maneuver illustrated, but rather to represent the stage of training

35

at which the particular horse was at the time of photographing.

The rule of thumb, as far as I'm concerned, is that one does not solve a training problem with a bit. A bit is a device used to help communicate our ideas to our horse and to be able to feel his communication to us. For example, a harsher bit does not produce a better stop; good basic schooling will produce the best stop.

So start with the snaffle and do not move into a transitional bit until the horse evidences calmness, straightness, collection, lateral control, smooth and quiet lead changes, and cued stops. If he doesn't understand in a snaffle bit (the mildest bit of them all), he won't understand when greater pressure is exerted on his mouth.

One last comment before we proceed into the meat of our subject: Although "the first saddling" sounds like the beginning of the horse's training, the process actually begins when he is born. The process itself is an ever-expanding spiral. I think that the best approach any of us can take is to always be willing to learn, and to realize how much we can learn from the horse.

I doubt if there is a man in America who has saddled as many colts as my friend Ray Hunt. He is beyond a doubt the absolute master at saddling an unbroke colt. The key to his success is his ability to foster mental relaxation in his pupil.   **Photo by Peter Phinny**

I doubt that there is a man in America who has saddled as many colts as my friend Ray Hunt, and most of those that he has started were extremely green, if not just plain wild. He is beyond a doubt the absolute master at saddling a green horse. I'll match him against any living human. Ray is able to not only saddle a bronc colt, he can do anything he wants with the colt after it has been saddled.

The key to Ray's success is his ability to foster mental relaxation in his pupil; his phenomenal results are based on the premise that we must remove fear from the horse's behavioral pattern. The best way to remove fear, in Ray's terms, is to impress on the colt the notion that we are his friend. After we have done this, and when he has placed his trust in us, we can saddle him readily and easily.

Years ago I felt that the only way to effectively saddle a green colt was to sideline or Scotch-hobble him. With one hind foot pulled off the ground and the horse in a semimobile condition, we were then free to sack the horse out and

For the first saddling, I like to work in a round pen. First, I rub him on the face, then back away. I repeat this until he indicates he enjoys it, then I begin rubbing him down his left side, as I'm doing here. **Photo by Peter Phinny**

After he stands quietly for the rubbing on the left side, I immediately do the same thing on his right side, starting with his head and neck and moving all the way back to his croup. **Photo by Peter Phinny**

force him to submit to the saddling process. Many horsemen still do it this way.

The horse, however, has a different viewpoint. He doesn't willingly submit, he is forced to submit. With this method we are trying to take the fear out of him, rather than trying never to create the fear, or to gain his trust.

The colt's background and how he was managed prior to the first saddling will have a big influence on how he will react. A barn-raised colt who has been in constant contact with people, one that shows no fear at the newness of the situation and surroundings, will be much easier to saddle for the first time. Actually, he has no fear motive and is not trying to escape. He might even be a little bit inquisitive about what's happening.

The colt that has run in pasture with other colts all his life, one that has not had contact with people, will react differently to the same set of circumstances.

It is the trainer's responsibility to evaluate the situation and the colt's background. This is called *reading the colt,* and if we do a good job it surely helps out the process. The important thing to remember is that the colt's behavior in a new situation will be closely linked to fear. A horse's natural reaction to fear is flight, and he will want to leave if he

Next, alternate between rubbing him and raising both arms into the air. Continue until he no longer flinches or moves away when you raise your arms. **Photo by Peter Phinny**

Now get a feed sack, hold it in front of you so he can see it (above), then rub him all over with it and also hold it overhead until he no longer pays any attention to it. **Photos by Peter Phinny**

doesn't understand what is happening.

Let me repeat that. He will want to leave, take to flight, if he doesn't understand what is happening. I didn't say that he would want to leave only if he felt pain, I said that he would want to leave if he didn't understand; this is a purely mental consideration. A wise trainer will constantly keep this in mind and will work any angle to remove the fear motive. Progress will depend on how well we manage in this area. To borrow one of Yogi Berra's famous non sequiturs from the baseball world, "Ninety-five percent of this game is half mental."

For the first saddling I think an enclosure, a small pen or a round pen, is best. A round pen is ideal; a box stall is the worst.

Take the colt into the pen with a halter and stand him quietly facing you. Walk directly toward him and rub his face. Back away, walk toward him, and rub his face again; however, don't rub him for long periods of time. Repeat this until he indicates that he enjoys it and does not back away or try to evade.

Next, walk toward him again and after rubbing his face continue rubbing his neck on the left side, then over his withers and down his back and croup. If he shows uneasiness, back off and start over. Remember, approach him with a positive attitude like, "Ol' pardner, this won't take a minute and you'll enjoy it."

After he stands quietly for the rubbing on the left side, do the same thing immediately on the right side. Alternate until he is completely satisfied and comfortable with the goings-on.

Next, as you work both sides, raise your arms into the air as you rub him. This will annoy him a little, but go to the other side and do the same thing until you can wave your arms over him as you proceed with the rubbing process. Usually this only takes a few minutes.

Try the same thing with a sack. Rub him with a sack and hold it overhead until he pays no attention to it. Soon you can wave it widely over his head and he will be completely indifferent to it.

He is now ready to be saddled. We have removed the fear behavior pattern. Take your saddle pad in hand and walk directly to him exactly as you did with the sack. Place the pad quietly on his back; now rub it up and down his back, over his withers, up his neck, and over his croup in a sliding motion. Do it from both sides in a deliberate motion, but not slowly. He will submit to this, he'll accept it.

Next comes the saddle. Make sure that the cinch and the right stirrup are fastened up and out of the way. Use the saddle exactly like the pad; place it on his back and gently move it left and right. Now walk to his right side, let the cinch down, and go back to his left side. Reach under for the cinch and gently let him feel it against his underside.

If he shows little or no concern, place the latigo in the cinch ring and slowly pull it up. When the cinch is snug enough to hold the saddle in place, stop. Now remove the lead rope, or half-hitch it over the saddle horn rather loosely, and step back.

Do not try to scare the colt out of his tracks, simply walk away from him. He will show some concern; he has a tight cinch under his belly and this is a new experience. He must figure out the situation for himself, and his first reaction will probably be to explode and buck around the pen. Leave him alone and allow him to figure out his situation; he will soon stop. Get out of the pen and leave him alone for half an hour or more. He will decide that this situation isn't all that bad and he has no real reason to be afraid.

After he has been allowed to work out his situation, re-enter the pen and repeat the rubbing process, then unsaddle him. Make sure that he faces you, and rub his face before you unsaddle. Keep everything quiet and deliberate. Make sure that he is not afraid, and that the process has been a reasonably pleasant experience for him. The important thing to remember during the first few saddling sessions is that the colt stand quietly during the process.

It is also important to become repetitious during the saddling sessions: try to do it the same way every time. If the horse becomes uneasy, settle him and softly start over. Time is unimportant, you don't have a schedule to keep. Constantly position him and don't place the saddle on him until he will stand. If you are careful in this respect, he will soon

Now take your saddle blanket, and hold it so he can see it. Place it on his back. Rub it up and down and back and forth from his withers to his croup. Do it from both sides—not slowly, but in a deliberate motion. When he stands quietly for this, you have removed the fear behavior pattern and he is ready to be saddled. **Photo by Peter Phinny**

Make sure the cinch, latigo, and right stirrup are fastened up and out of the way. **Photo by Peter Phinny**

Ease the saddle onto his back.

Before cinching up, gently move the saddle back and forth and from one side to the other.

Photos by Peter Phinny

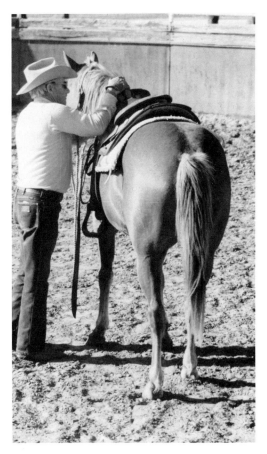

stand quietly each time you saddle him because he doesn't know that there is any other way.

Make it a pleasant experience for him. If after saddling you take a few seconds to walk around him and reward him by rubbing and petting him, he will wait for it. If you are careful about the first ten saddlings, future saddlings will take care of themselves; he will never move a foot. It is the mark of a broke horse.

If you have to chase the horse all over the pen to get the saddle on, there is something wrong and it is not the horse. Your horse should stand quietly to be saddled. If you need to put him in cross-ties or tie him in order to saddle him, he just ain't broke, pardner. Also, don't forget to work both sides of the horse; he should saddle as well from one side as the other.

During the saddling process, nearly all horsemen are guilty of one glaring mistake. They cinch a horse too tightly. On the initial saddling, only snug up the cinch; don't cut the colt in two. He is in an entirely new situation and to make him uncomfortable with a tight cinch only invites problems. The horse tells us that he is uncomfortable when he switches his tail, twists, turns, and is obviously under some kind of stress. Watch for the signals.

After we are riding him, he tells us even more. He can't perform if he is being bothered by something he is unable to do anything about. Imagine telling a pro athlete that he can perform better if we tighten his belt four notches, or that if we further tighten our neckties we will enjoy the banquet more.

Only in some working events, such as

Do not try to scare the colt out of his tracks; simply walk away. He will show some concern because the tight cinch is a new experience. He must figure out the situation for himself, and his first reaction will probably be to explode and buck around the pen. **Photo by Peter Phinny**

When he shows little or no concern, slowly cinch him up. When you feel that the cinch is snug enough to hold the saddle in place, either remove the halter or half-hitch the lead rope over the saddle horn rather loosely, and step back. **Photo by Peter Phinny**

roping, will you need to cinch up a little tighter than normal. If your saddle fits so badly you must cinch tightly to hold it in place, get another saddle. Show me a horse cinched too loosely, and I'll show you one that will perform a heck of a lot better than one cinched too tightly.

Note: The first few times you saddle a colt, do not turn him loose in a round pen unless it has a fence at least 6½ feet high. Otherwise, if he reacts violently to the saddle, he might try to jump out of the pen.

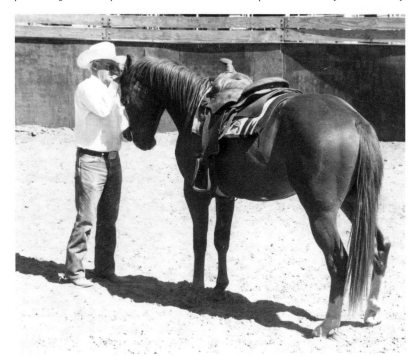

This last picture is of a different colt who had been saddled for the first time. After he quit bucking, quieted down, and realized there was no reason to be afraid, I re-entered the pen. I walked up to him and rubbed his face before I unsaddled him.

41

5 WHERE ARE WE HEADED?

What is it that we want in a broke horse? Ask 10 horsemen and you will get 10 different answers.

I have schooled horses for a lifetime and probably the biggest lesson I have learned is that I am woefully ignorant. I know that there is always a positive way to solve whatever dilemma I am facing; there is always an effective way for my horse and for me, and my job is to find it.

I am convinced that there never should be problems in the first place.

They arise, in my estimation, because of misunderstandings between the horse and his rider. I am equally convinced that these misunderstandings are 99 percent the rider's fault, my fault. Pitifully few riders give the horse even a hint of consideration when they issue their cues or wishes, let alone study their horse's reaction to them. Trainers seem to expect immediate, gratifying response regard-

As we work our horses, we should continually think about them performing perfectly. Before we make a run-down for a sliding stop, for example, we should envision our horse in perfect position and making a flawless slide. A rider should even position his/her body as though stopping the world's greatest sliding horse. This is Kim Diercks, my former assistant trainer, sliding her fine mare, Okies Juliet.

Photo by Peter Phinny

less of whether or not the cues issued were correct or on time. We, as trainers, too often appear sure that the cues we issued were the ones needed. The ignorance of too many trainers is appalling. Some train by absolute force and constantly search for ways and gimmicks to inflict pain or discomfort on their horses in order to make them respond. Watch the practice ring at any horse show if you want to be further reminded of this. If one of these trainers has a problem, it is always the horse's fault, never his own. I hear excuses by the dozens, but the horse is always the goat.

From a humane standpoint, how can we change this situation? What can we do for the horse? Let's analyze it a little.

With our modern performance-bred horses (and make no doubt about it, they are good ones), 99 percent of them should be willing pupils; they all want to learn. In addition, 95 percent of them are athletic enough to perform challenging maneuvers. All horses aren't the same, of course, but this is the basic material most trainers have to start with.

But what is their success rate? Probably 10 percent. Why? I'll very candidly tell you why. It is trainer ignorance. Now, don't misunderstand me, I'm included. I know that there is always a good way to get our message across to our colts and horses, and I think that we should constantly be working at this kind of communication.

I also know that healthy communication is not accomplished by bridle, spur, gimmick, and force. Horses don't like to be completely dominated every minute that they carry a rider. They, like all of us, want to express themselves, and we need to let them.

I feel that we must form a partnership and a friendship with our horses; we must trust one another, and we must not violate this trust. Both partners must depend on the other and work together as a team. Not only must they work together, they must think together toward a common goal. This is like learning a dance with a partner.

In this team effort the trainer must constantly consider how his partner feels about the situation. Since his partner is a silent one, however, the rider must ask his questions in many ways. When he issues a cue, he must study the response from his partner the horse. From his observation he must learn whether or not the communication is mutual. If he is reasonably sure that the cue or command is in order and was issued at the right time but he gets a negative response, then it is time to reissue and to wait for a more positive response.

To paraphrase Ray Hunt, "We should be able to notice the slightest change and to reward the slightest try." I have to believe that the majority of problems would never have been problems at all if the trainer was more observant.

Nearly all trainers forget that their greatest asset in the entire process is their power of observation. Few even bother with it. If we watch our horses, they will tell us. In fact, they are desperately trying to tell us. One horse might be telling us that he doesn't understand algebra because he has only had fifth-grade arithmetic. If we want him to understand algebra, we better finish the arithmetic first. One thing, nevertheless, is certain: Our horse will communicate with us somehow, and we must be prepared to listen.

The greatest horseman in America, in my estimation, is Ray Hunt's teacher, Tom Dorrance. Tom says: "Don't forget that the horse is always right." Tom also says: "I'll be the horse's lawyer every time, and I'll win 99 percent of the cases." He is so right. Always defend your horse.

I often hear trainers tell one another how they solved a horse's problem by "getting into his mind." You would think that they had completed their Ph.D. in animal psychology, or that they were behavioral scientists. I'd like to hear the horse's version of these mind games.

Throughout history horsemen have realized that many of the better riders have psychological qualities which enable them to have an inner contact with their horses, and that these horsemen ride horses showing great obedience. This type of alliance between horse and rider is a telepathy of the spirit, and it is a level of understanding above that of a trainer attempting in a one-sided way to "get into his horse's mind."

We also occasionally see a horseman with an uncanny ability to communicate with his horses and we define it by saying, "He's a natural."

Patience, inexhaustible patience, is necessary to make the horse understand what we want of him. Patience is also equally necessary in order not to grow immoderately demanding. Here, I am trying to communicate with my horse, and am working to direct one foot at a time. I'm a fanatic about foot position.

Waldemar Seunig, the fabulous German horseman and author, describes in his book *Horsemanship* (©1956, Doubleday and Co.) a rider's psychological abilities. He says, " . . . a rider has three psychological resources: 1/ Love of the horse; 2/ Mental equilibrium; and 3/ Energy."

In Seunig's estimation, love of the horse is the most important, and with that a horse will overcome its inborn shyness and gain confidence (which is a fundamental condition for mutual understanding) with a man whose love it feels. Anyone who loves his horse will be patient—and patience, inexhaustible patience, is necessary to make the horse understand what we want of him. Patience is also equally necessary in order not to grow immoderately demanding.

The second element is mental equilibrium. To be in psychological equilibrium as a rider, one must have a sure understanding of what, and of how much, can

be asked of a horse in any period of time. One must also have a sure understanding of when it can be asked, based on one's own conscious feelings. The rider must comprehend the natural limits of what a particular horse can do.

An understanding of this balance will keep an angry rider from excessive punishment which would, in turn, destroy the confidence the horse has in his rider. If the rider has the gift of correct and appropriate diagnosis (discussed later in this chapter), and if he uses it in concert with understanding, he will be able to handle whatever job he has to do in the saddle.

Energy is the last of Seunig's psychological resources, and whenever we become involved in a struggle with a horse, we must constantly devote energy to overcoming the problem. We're talking here not about using force, but using creative energy—devoting energy to figuring out the particular dilemma. Sometimes this requires us to try and try again before we get the slightest response. Many times we are tempted to give up, but it is the stay-with-it attitude that produces success. This is where the use of our energy becomes a factor.

Keeping this in mind, as long as we combine some measure of diplomacy with our concentrated energy (as well as Seunig's other psychological resources), we will have a good chance of success. Few people who are successful in any endeavor got there without devoting energy and hard work.

Maxwell Maltz, although not writing specifically about horses in his book *Psycho-Cybernetics* (©1960, Prentice-Hall, Inc.), develops theories which can help us manifest these psychological resources talked about by Seunig.

The message in *Psycho-Cybernetics*, in effect, is that we can *think* a thing into happening, and that in an effort to realize our goal, we must first envision the goal as already ours. We constantly think, think, think about our objective as being realized.

I am a firm believer in this theory. I feel that, as we work our horse, we should continually think about him performing perfectly. For example, before we make a run-down for a sliding stop, we should envision our horse in perfect position and doing a flawless slide. A

44

The greatest asset we have in the entire process of training a horse is our power of observation. When a trainer issues a cue, he must study the response from his partner the horse. If we watch the horse, he will tell us if he understands what we want. Constantly observe your horse in an effort to understand his responses. I'm asking this horse to turn to the left.

rider should even arrange his body and issue cues as though stopping the world's greatest sliding horse. Think about doing it correctly each time you signal, cue, or set up your horse for a maneuver.

I am a firm believer in mental telepathy, and I know that you can think yourself onto the same wavelength as your horse, especially if you are friends and if you trust one another. Also, you must believe in your horse. If you ride your horse wondering whether or not he is going to perform the maneuver correctly, he'll most likely do it wrong; he won't disappoint you.

If he performed incorrectly—that is, if the result of his maneuver was something other than what you wanted—the chances are that you didn't issue positive cues and follow up with the support he needed to do it correctly.

The bottom line is to think. Few of us do. Remember, the horse is always right. If he performs something wrong, he is only telling us that we didn't get our message across. If our horse doesn't do what we want, or what we think he should do, our first reaction should be to immediately analyze the situation, and

we do this by thinking and questioning.

We ask ourselves what happened. What are the contributing factors? Is this a mistake or a confirmed habit? Is the problem mental, physical, or a combination of both? Are we demanding too much or not enough? Has he been punished for this in the past? Does he need to be punished? Are there alternatives to this situation? If one treatment doesn't work, do we have another to try in its place? Do we need to back off? Did we bypass the basics?

Don't forget that the greatest resource any of us has to help solve a problem lies underneath one's own hat.

Schooling a horse hinges not only on properly handling hundreds of situations but, more fundamentally, on the ability to see and understand the real cause of any difficulty encountered by the horse. Throughout history there have been many great horsemen, many who could do unbelievable things with a horse. Natural or born horsemen they were called, and their mental, physical, and psychological qualities set them apart from other trainers. They had the unique ability to do exactly the right thing at

exactly the right time, and they understood the psychological state of the
horse with which they were working.

The God-given gift which perhaps
most exemplifies the natural horseman is
his ability to diagnose. What could be
more important? It's the same in the
medical profession. What makes one
doctor better than another? Probably his
ability to diagnose, the understanding to
know what he is dealing with.

I am convinced that diagnosis for a
horseman is an inborn gift and that great
horsemen have it. We all have an ability
to diagnose to some degree or another,
and without a doubt all but the truly
gifted must strive to develop this sense.
Correct diagnosis is always half the solution. Good doctors don't become skilled
making bad diagnoses, and neither will
trainers. Learn to recognize the real
cause of a problem. Remove the cause
and you have effected the cure. This
should be etched on every horse trainer's
barn wall.

Anything we do with a horse, in any
situation or in any event, is based on
control of that horse. If we are to direct
the horse's body, we must have control
of all of its parts. This is the area in
which most of us are lax. We simply
don't adequately control all the parts—
the legs, shoulders, feet, rib cage, back—
all those elements that when focused
precisely result in complete communication and hence control.

Sometimes we are lucky and find natural horses who are great ones and require half the training it takes the others.
These horses seem to train themselves.
With these rare individuals we are then
consequently lulled into thinking that all
horses should train this way and, as a
result, we try to take short cuts. With
short cuts we skip the basics, and without the basics we eventually get into big
trouble. This is as foolhardy as building
a nice house on a partially built
foundation.

Since control is what we are after, we
must faithfully teach control. When we
school for collection, it is control of the
head, neck, and ultimately the back and
hindquarters. When we school for lead
changes, stops, etc., we concentrate on
control of the horse's feet. Only when we
control the parts can we then exercise
control of the body. I'm talking here

about the basic elements of movement;
they must be taught one at a time at a
rate that the horse comprehends.

We will address fundamental maneuvers in subsequent chapters, but for
now, while focusing on control, store
away in your mind the notion that two
keys to success in schooling for control
of the horse's various parts are calmness
and softness. Whenever we demand too
strongly with spur or rein, our horse will
tighten up; he will become tense and
block us out mentally because he is more
concerned with the punishment than
with understanding our cues. So keep
your actions soft. Ask, don't demand.

If we stress softness, our horse soon
becomes accustomed to it; he wants to
be soft, to be supple, and we are then
able to repeatedly ask for correctness
and position. If a horse understands a
soft approach, the training exercises
become easy and he will not become
overly stressed when we ask him for
more, when we challenge him more.

An important thing to remember in
the training process is to keep the finished product in mind. We should remain goal-oriented, so to speak. Don't
get into the habit of training just to train.
We must envision our trainee as a finished horse doing exactly as the world
champions do. In our mind's eye, we
should see him winning the big one.

Another important consideration
takes the form of a series of questions
and involves a definition of terms: What
is a "broke" horse? What are his trade-
marks? What can he do? Ask 10 horsemen these questions and you will get 10
different answers.

Dressage people have a pretty good
idea because they are governed by rigid
requirements and must perform satisfac-
torily at progressive levels. When their
horses reach the Grand Prix level, they
can do a lot and they are surely broke
horses from the control standpoint.
These horses are beautiful to watch and
they exemplify correctness.

We in the western horse world are
somewhat less exacting. We can compete
in many events, several timed, and our
ideas vary as to form and correctness.
We are judged differently than are dressage horses, and there is a wide variance
of individual opinion among judges.
Our horses tend to be specialized, and

*If we stress softness, our horse soon becomes accustomed to it; he
wants to be soft, to be supple, and we are then able to repeatedly ask
for correctness and position. Because Kim has been soft with this
3-year-old colt, she can continually work on straightness and correct
positioning without causing the colt any stress. She's asking, not
demanding. Kim is working on the colt's turn-around.*

most are single-event horses. We often
see outstanding horses in one event that,
when asked to compete in another event,
are disasters. When we do see a good
horse compete in several events, which is
becoming rare, we naturally tend to
consider him a well-broke horse.

I feel that if we concentrate on the
basics, spend more time on control,
softness, and on such things as head and
foot position, we will all be riding better-
broke horses.

Happily, this brings us full circle to the
question from which the title of this
chapter is drawn: Where are we headed
with our training? What is it that we
want in a broke horse?

My response has to be personal. I feel
a horse must be proficient in several
areas for him to be classified as a broke
horse. If your horse performs these
movements well, and if you have complete control of all of them and of the
elements that make them up, then I am
confident that your horse will be considered broke by anyone.

The following are the areas I want to
stress, and consequently they represent
the titles of the next six chapters: calmness, straightness, collection, lateral
control, lead changes, and stops.

6　CALMNESS

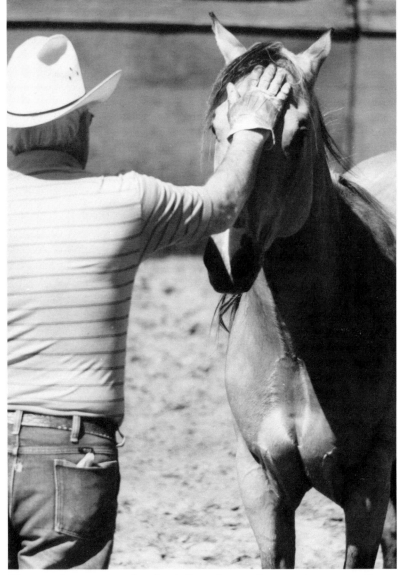

The very best way, and perhaps the only genuine way, to remove the fear motive is to gain the horse's confidence and trust, and the best way to do this is to make friends with him. In all our work with and around our horse, we need to reward him so that he looks forward to our presence rather than anticipating ways to evade us.　**Photo by Peter Phinny**

The first, and most important, prerequisite for a horse, in order to make the training process productive, is calmness. Even an amateur knows the difference between a quiet, calm horse and a nervous, flighty, wild-eyed, and excitable one. Quiet horses train more easily, require less discipline, and definitely last longer than frightened, nervous horses. It is that simple. Calm horses are the result of heredity, handling, and environment. In our training sessions we need to always keep our horses calm.

What do we do when we encounter a young horse who in all other areas is adequate, but who doesn't have the quiet, calm attitude that we'd like? Our first approach should be to watch the horse closely and to try to determine the root of the problem. Is his nervousness related to heredity, handling, or environment? There is a pretty good chance that we can improve the situation if we can determine the cause.

Most horses exhibit nervousness because of fear. Since a horse has an excellent memory, some incident in the past might be triggering the problem. The very best way, and perhaps the only genuine way, to remove the fear motive is to gain the horse's confidence and trust. The best way to do this is to make friends with him. In all our work with and around our horse, we need to reward him so he looks forward to our presence rather than anticipating ways to evade us. This effort should begin any time we come in contact with our horse. If we rub him, pat him, scratch him as often as we can, he will soon decide that our presence is okay.

48

What happens if our horse wants to charge, bolt, run, or shows no willingness to relax when we ride him? Take him into a small pen (a round pen is best), get on him with a halter and lead rope, and let him go wherever he pleases. Do not pull on the lead rope.

Now, what happens when he still wants to charge, bolt, run, or if he shows no willingness to relax when we ride him? This is fun as well as a challenge. Saddle him and take him into a small pen. A round pen is best. Get on him with a halter and lead rope only. Do not try to pull on the lead rope. Completely throw him away and let him go wherever he pleases. Just go along for the ride. Constantly pet and reward him, and let him go freestyle.

If you are in a round pen, let him lope on his own accord until he decides to walk. Now start to softly direct him with the lead rope. Stay out of his way until you feel him relax. His body movements will soften, his head carriage will lower, and he will allow you to apply some leg pressure against his sides.

When he relaxes, whether it takes two days of half-hour sessions or two weeks (and time is not a factor, don't worry about time), repeat the exercises in the round pen with your horse in some kind of snaffle bit; an O-ring, D-ring, eggbutt, or full-cheek snaffle would be fine. If, after a few sessions of this soft riding, he is showing signs of relaxation, take him to a bigger enclosure. Then if he shows tenseness, walk him until he re-laxes before moving to a faster gait.

If he gets excited at any stage, always drop back the level of pressure until you feel relaxation, then ask him again. It is futile to pull on his face with the reins; that is an invitation for more tenseness and charging.

Repeatedly, after a quieting session, start back at an extended trot; after the horse trots smoothly on a light rein, break him into a lope. Let him lope for a limited number of strides, and then drop him back to the trot. Each time lope a little farther, using a loose rein of course, before dropping back to the trot. Always wind up your training with a quiet walking session. Think "relax," and the horse will start to relax.

When using the reins, only hint with them. Don't pull on them. Remember, pulling on the reins is a definite invitation for the horse to push against the bit and to charge. When all else fails, go back to the walk. You are never wrong walking quietly. He sure as heck won't lope quietly if he won't walk quietly.

Years ago I operated a horse rental stable. We offered one-hour rides along a wooded trail. All rides were at the walk, and they were accompanied by a trail leader. The riders were predomi-

49

Just go along for the ride. Let him lope or trot on his own accord until he decides to walk.

Stay out of his way until you feel him relax. His body movements will soften, his head carriage will lower, he will allow you to apply some leg pressure against his sides without over-reacting, and you can softly direct him with the lead rope.

nantly beginners and kids, and consequently the horses were the quietest available.

Whenever we had a nervous, hyper horse in our adjoining training stable, we immediately sent him down to the rental division for the trail leader to ride. After several trips up the trail daily at the walk, the results were unbelievable. Everything was at the walk on a loose rein and surrounded by quiet horses. No hurry, no pulling on his mouth; a completely relaxed atmosphere with repeated trips up the same trail.

One month of this and the nervous horse was almost transformed into a dog. The nervous horse became as quiet as the rest of the rental horses. Why? Because we put him into an entirely calm, relaxed frame of mind, and we didn't call on him for anything. It worked every time. If you want a horse to calm down, ride calmly.

During our training sessions in general, there are several approaches that we can take that tend to produce calmness in an excitable horse. Probably first and foremost is that we need to ride him. In this age, it seems that we have completely forgotten that a horse is designed to carry a rider and saddle for at least an eight-hour period.

We all know what the Pony Express riders could do with their horses. Indians like the Cheyenne and the Sioux could ride their horses for miles and miles and then chase buffalo with them. Remember, too, that these ponies were all under 15 hands and surely were not grain-fed.

Now we have big, solid, grain-fed, stall-bound horses with lots of energy, and we think they should come out of the stall ready to lope off quietly and calmly. It will rarely happen. But in most instances, the more we ride them the calmer they will become.

Small training areas, show rings, or arenas are poor places to put miles on a horse. In these environments the horse must constantly work in a circle and he soon becomes bored. He becomes bored not from the training area alone, but

When the horse finally decides to stop, just sitting on him and allowing him to relax will promote calmness. When you can feel that he's relaxed, repeat the same procedure, but this time with a snaffle bit.

from the fact that he is cramped in his way of moving. Constant circles promote all kinds of body misalignment. Get out of the arena . . . go someplace.

A few years ago one of my assistant trainers complained about a mare he was riding. She absolutely would not quiet down, he told me. I then asked how much he had ridden her. He told me that he was on her constantly. I then suggested that he saddle her and take her down the highway in the bar-ditch.

"How far?" he asked.

"Ride her to Winona," I told him, "and I'll be down tonight and pick you up."

Winona was 35 miles away. "You've got to be kidding," he exclaimed.

"Get going," I told him, "she'll be quieter tonight."

That night I picked my assistant and the mare up after their 35-mile hike and

Wet saddle blankets acquired while *going somewhere* will do more to instill calmness in a horse than almost anything.

If the colt shows any signs of tenseness, walk him until he relaxes before moving to a faster gait. If he gets excited at any stage, always drop the level of pressure until you feel him relax.

she was definitely quiet. We brought her home, and the next morning I started him out again down the same highway, but I picked him up after only 15 miles. The mare was a new horse. She had gotten used to the traffic, noise, obstacles, everything. Nothing fazed her. She hadn't been abused, only ridden, and it changed her whole attitude. She would lope off softly on a loose rein with no idea of running. Wet saddle blankets acquired while *going somewhere* will do more to instill calmness in a horse than almost anything.

Just plain sitting on your horse also tends to promote quietness. After a brief workout, stop your horse and allow him to stand on a loose rein. Do absolutely nothing other than to pet his neck a little. Wait for him to drop his head, and when he does, give him a slight rub along the neck or behind the saddle on his hips. Remember, you are promoting calmness, so be calm. Soon your horse will look forward to this rest period and this is the attitude you are after. Following the rest period always walk off and stay at a calm walk for at least a short period of time.

While we're on the subject of walking, let me suggest another good technique: Walk your horse the entire training session. Do not even break him into a slow trot. Only walk. Walk him 180 degrees over his hocks and walk off in the opposite direction. Next time, turn a full 360 degrees and again walk, but only on a loose rein. Walk the entire session, and then put him up just as if you had worked him heavily.

Later in the day give him another session of the same treatment. He'll remember repetition. If he has had two or even three sessions in one day at the walk, he will look forward to it. Watch your horse and study his reaction to the situation. We want him to have pleasant thoughts about his training.

Another technique is to break up the routine to which he has become accustomed. Most nervous horses are full of anticipation. They know as soon as we head for the training area that it will be a repeat of yesterday's happenings. Today, saddle up and get ready the same as yesterday, only don't ride him immediately. Instead, tie him to the fence and let him watch while others are schooling.

Once he is relaxed, ask him to lope again.

Let him stand for two or three hours, and then get on and reverse the schedule. Walk him, stop and rest, or get off, lead him over to the fence, retie him, and go do something else. Do exactly the opposite of that to which he is accustomed, but always quietly and softly.

Make sure as you work around the horse that you pet him. Keep impressing on him that there is an easy way for him to cope with whatever is bothering him, and that you are his relief. If you really watch and observe him with your intuitive sense, he will show you what he's thinking.

If in our riding session a horse shows signs of extreme nervousness, and if he constantly wants to speed up rather than relax, our first concern should be to determine why. What causes this reaction, this problem? To make this discovery we should go back to the basics; we are trying to find the cause in order to effect the cure. Perhaps the problem is hereditary. Maybe it's environmental. If he has been ridden by another rider, it could be past history.

We also had better check our equipment. Perhaps his bridle isn't comfort-able, or the curb chain is too tight, or the browband is rubbing his ear. Maybe there is not enough padding under the saddle. Don't forget a chief cause for a horse's discomfort: a cinch drawn up too tightly.

Any one of dozens of minor problems can cause an abnormal or stressful attitude in a horse. If we can find out why the horse has a problem, it is a lot easier to fix than if we reprimand the horse without knowing why he is failing to function as we would like him to. Remember: *Remove the cause and you have effected a cure.*

Something else important to remember is that our softness and kindness with horses must not be only in the training pen. Many trainers ride their horses, put them away, and have no more contact with them until the next session. It is much better if we associate with them a little more often, especially while they are in the stall, pen, or at the hitching post.

Each time we come in contact with them, it should be on the same old friendly basis. If we enter the stall with them several times a day, even if only for

When using the reins, only hint with them; don't pull on them. Remember: Pulling on the reins (particularly in the early going or when the horse is tense) allows the horse to push against the bit and charge. When all else fails, go back to the walk.

Just plain sitting on your horse also tends to promote quietness. After a brief workout, stop your horse and allow him to stand on a loose rein. Do nothing, except to pet his neck a little. Wait for him to drop his head and when he does, give him a slight rub along the neck or on his hips.

Small training areas, arenas, and show rings are poor places to put miles on a horse. In those situations the horse must constantly work in circles and he soon becomes bored and cramped in his way of moving. Constant circles promote all kinds of body misalignment. Get out of the arena—go someplace.

a few minutes to rub them, brush them, or to pick up their feet, then their confidence in us will grow, and we will be working on the cure for their nervousness and uncertainty. It is amazing how a horse's attitude will change when he begins to feel at ease with us.

Many trainers spend too much time training and too little time just softly riding their horses. I realize that the professional trainer has to accomplish as much as he can on a colt or horse in a limited amount of time, but we must remember that the horse might not be on the same time schedule as we are, and that pushing too fast might cause the beginning of a variety of problems. Let the horse tell you when he is ready to advance; if you know your horse, you'll realize when he is comfortable and confident in one stage and ready to try the next. It takes two to tango.

The trainer who is constantly picking at his horse and forever correcting him is in for trouble somewhere along the line. If the horse isn't confused at first, he soon will be, and after becoming confused he will hunt for ways to evade rather than comply. The good trainer searches for ways to make the training session fun; he doesn't "power" his horses through their maneuvers. I'd lots rather have the horse give me his attention and try hard, rather than try to force him to pay attention to me.

All trainers at every level of training should remember to keep calmness in mind. It's one of the keys to progress. Good trainers pay attention to a colt's attitude and watch for signs and indications as to how the horse feels. He indicates his feelings in unmistakable terms with his eyes, his ears, and with his tail. Pay attention to them.

7 STRAIGHTNESS

Being able to keep his body straight is important in almost every maneuver we ask the horse to do.

When a horse travels straight, his hind feet follow his front feet in the same vertical plane. As a consequence, his weight is evenly loaded on all four legs; even loading is absolutely necessary for a horse to perform properly. Here, I'm loping between two parallel strings and although we are starting out decently, I need to move him off my right leg a little to get him straighter.

Far too many trainers pay far too little attention to the straightness factor during the schooling program. Maintaining straightness in your horse is basic, and executing it cures a myriad of problems. Let's explore it a little.

When a horse travels straight, his hind feet follow his front feet in the same vertical plane. As a consequence, his weight is evenly loaded on all four of his legs; even loading is absolutely necessary for

a horse to function optimally. I need to once again pay tribute to the German horseman I mentioned previously, Waldemar Seunig, who, in his book *Horsemanship*, very succinctly describes what I have referred to as even loading.

"For a horse to move in equestrian balance," Seunig writes, "the burden must be uniformly shared by each pair of legs, each front leg carrying exactly half of the load on the forehand, and each hind leg carrying exactly half the load on the hindquarters, so that the horse is in complete lateral balance. When a horse goes crooked with his hind feet failing to track the front feet, he is not in equestrian balance and his suppleness will be incomplete because it is not based on the even extension of the groups of muscles on the right and left halves of the horse's body."

All right, so why is straightness so important, and what happens without it? To answer this question, let's put a horse in a few "unstraight" positions and analyze him.

As the first example, consider loping in a circle as required by all reining patterns, or a large oval as in a pleasure class. If the horse is not straight, his outside hind foot (the driver in this case) is stepping wide or to the outside of the intended circle. He is evading with his foot. When he thus evades, he falls against the rider's outside leg, against the inside rein, and heavily on the inside shoulder. In reining horse jargon, he "drops his shoulder."

What do most reiners do to correct this situation? They immediately lift the inside rein to raise him off the dropped shoulder. This is the wrong end to work on. The dropped shoulder is caused by the evading outside driving hind foot. This is where the problem could have been prevented. Always remember that if you remove the cause you have effected a cure.

Tom Dorrance, whom I have also referred to earlier in this book, says it this way: "Pay attention to his back end, and the front end will take care of itself." How right he is. Our circling horse needs to know how to move with his body straight and therefore evenly loaded.

Another example: Suppose that we are teaching our horse to stop, and we are loping him quietly down our stopping area or sliding track. For some reason our horse is not straight; he is loping in two tracks, or perhaps he wants to bear left or right during a straight run, or he runs with his head canted to the right or left. The point is that for some reason our horse is not longitudinally straight.

Now we ask for the stop, and what happens? He slams into the ground sideways, flexing one hock and not the other. Since he is not balanced and straight, his head is apt to go anywhere, but it will probably go up. Possibly one hind foot will slide a little, but his stop will be a series of stiff-legged bounces.

His tracks will look more like a series of exclamation points than the figure eleven that indicates correct balance and alignment. The unsatisfactory stop resulted because the horse was not straight. Anyone who has tried to stop a crooked horse will understand what I am talking about.

When you expect your horse to stop straight, make sure that he is properly prepared. Send him toward his stop with his body straight and evenly loaded, and his head and neck out in front, not up in the air or canted to the right or left.

This straightness is pure prerequisite. If your horse isn't straight or in balance, don't try to stop him. Turn around and try again; constantly frame your horse between your legs and reins until he is straight, and then ask for the stop. His legs, body, and neck must be in alignment in order to make it easier for him. Pay attention to him.

Another example: In this case we are teaching our colt to spin. We have succeeded in getting him to step across in

If the horse is not straight while loping circles, his outside hind foot (the left here) steps wide to the outside of the intended circle. This results in his pushing against the rider's outside leg, leaning against the inside rein, and dropping his inside shoulder. Notice the strain this is putting on his right front foot.

For whatever reason, this horse was not straight when he was asked to stop. What happened? He slammed into the ground crooked, with one hock flexed and the other one straight. His stop will be a series of stiff-legged bounces instead of one smooth slide.

Kim is teaching this colt to spin. He is stepping across in front nicely, placing his outside (right) forefoot in front of the inside foot. But in hurrying him a little, Kim is legging harder with her outside (right) leg and is leading him with the inside rein, which has resulted in the colt's body becoming crooked. To maintain his balance, the colt will have to pick up and reposition his pivot foot (left hind), and this will result in his hindquarters moving to the right. None of this would happen if the colt's body was straight.

front, placing his outside forefoot in front of his inside forefoot. Now we decide to hurry him a little, so we leg harder with our outside leg and we lead with our inside rein. The horse responds by resisting the rider's leg and "heavying up" on the leading rein, canting his head to the inside.

The only thing that we have succeeded in doing has been to hurry the colt into a crooked position. He will most likely do one of two things, and perhaps both. He will start to rise up or rear around in the turn, thereby losing the secure placement of his hindquarters, or he will try to step with his hindquarters in the direction of the turn and lose his pivot foot. Why? Because we crowded him and he lost his balance and longitudinal straightness.

I can cite example after example of situations and mistakes our horses constantly make because they are not

If your horse isn't straight or in balance when you are making a run-down, don't try to stop him. Just slow down, turn around, and try it again.

Your horse will enjoy going straight if given the opportunity. Ride him with some float in the reins; you do not have to keep contact with the bit. Allow him to relax; teach him that straightness and relaxation can be one and the same.

If your horse veers off, or if you feel a crook in his body, your hands and legs should automatically correct him. Soon, he will look where you look, and will travel straight.

How do we school for straightness? By riding in straight lines. Nearly all horses will go straight if given the opportunity, and if ridden outside. Pick out a distant object, and head straight for it.

straight. So many problems we face with our horses would not be problems at all if we had schooled longer in the basics, and keeping a horse straight is basic.

All right, how do we school for straightness? The answer is deceptively simple. We ride in straight lines. Nearly all horses will go straight if given an opportunity, so we must concentrate and feel our horse. If his body and spine are straight, he is even-loaded and his gait will be pure.

The best way, in my estimation, to school for straightness is to pick out a distant object—a tree, a telephone pole, anything in the distance—and fix your eyes on it. Ride directly at the object and do not watch your horse; *feel* your horse and watch only the object. If your horse veers off, your hands will automatically make the correction and soon the horse will look where you do, and he will go straight.

Constantly frame your horse between the reins and your legs until he is straight, and then ask for the stop. His legs, body, and neck must be aligned to make nice stops like this one.

If you have a large area in which to ride, the exercise becomes easier. To ride across a large field or pasture in a straight line is more conducive to straightness than across a small pen or arena.

Start this program at a walk, then a trot. Do not pick at your horse or constantly correct and rein back and forth. Don't overcontrol. Let it happen, don't make it happen. Your horse will enjoy going straight if given the opportunity. Ride your horse with some float in the reins; you do not have to maintain contact. Allow him to relax; teach him that straightness and relaxation can be one and the same.

I am a firm believer that one of the biggest mistakes trainers make is to always lope their horses in circles. Nothing destroys straightness like circles. When a horse lopes in a circle, the centrifugal force alone causes him to step to the outside with his outside or driving hind leg. He then immediately drops his inside shoulder, and he has lost his straightness.

If you are determined to lope circles, lope six-sided ones. Lope a few strides straight, then move your horse inside for a few strides, and so on. These are hexagon-shaped circles, which are really a series of straight lines. Even a D-shaped circle is better than a continually round pattern. Just give your horse a chance to get straight.

This discussion of circles is worth reinforcing. Don't forget that crookedness is produced by one hind leg evading the uncomfortable job of attempting to move in balance in a circle, and by the horse not advancing his leg underneath his frame, but somewhat off to one side. A result of this evasion is a bending of the horse's body that departs from the direction of the motion. So, ride your horse forward and keep him straight. Give him a chance to achieve straightness. Think about it.

You must develop a feel for body alignment. It must become instinctive, and you must be in tune with it at all times, in the same way that rein manipulation becomes second nature.

Do you ever see a rancher lope circles to get from one point to another? Ranch horses, that are allowed to lope straight all their lives, probably could run precise, pretty circles if asked because their bodies are always positioned for straightness.

An important thing to remember is that we shouldn't have schooling sessions for straightness as we think they are needed; instead, we should keep our horses straight at all times. We simply never let them travel crookedly. This must become a way of life for horse and rider. When a trainer has the control of all the parts, as this book advocates, it becomes easier and easier to keep the horse's body in alignment. When it

An important thing to remember is that we shouldn't have specific schooling sessions for straightness. Keeping a horse straight should be an integral part of every schooling session, as well as anytime we ride him. Here, Kim is backing a 4-year-old gelding. He is moving off the bit quietly, and Kim has "framed" him with the reins and her legs to keep him straight.

becomes a habit for the rider, he automatically reacts to the horse's body becoming out of line, and he executes the corrections almost unknowingly. Work to form the habit.

Obviously the most effective stage at which to instill straightness in our horses is at the beginning. A colt started straight is much more apt to remain that way than one who is allowed to lope circles too soon. Straightness is basic; it is by far the most important of the basic elements. Do not downplay it, because not to have it is an invitation to all kinds of unwanted and unexpected problems that could have been avoided.

At any gathering of mounted riders at a horse show, especially in the practice pen, pay attention to the horses you see who can move across the open space in a straight line. Look for the horses that hold their heads and necks in front and move evenly loaded. I'll guarantee there won't be many.

Why? Because few riders concentrate on straightness unless it becomes a major problem. Few really understand how important it is, or how much bearing it has on all the other aspects of a training program. Many, many trainers correct the results of "unstraightness" by pounding a horse in one part of its body or another, failing to even realize that quiet straightening of the horse's body position would remove the cause.

You must develop a feel for body alignment. It must become instinctive, and you must be in tune with it at all times, in the same way that rein manipulation becomes second nature.

Since their horses are judged on straightness, dressage riders are cognizant of it; they have an acute understanding of how important body alignment is in order to school for the other movements they teach their horses. For dressage riders, as it should be for all of us, straightness is everything.

Many times I have asked a rider about the straightness in his horse. His first reaction usually is, "Whudda ya mean straight?" After I explain, he then replies, "Oh, I don't have any trouble with that." Even though the horse he is riding might not be able to lope down a 20-foot alleyway, he is unaware of the root of the problem. The sad part of this common reaction is that many horse trainers aren't even remotely acquainted with the subject of straightness.

If you're in doubt about my harping on straightness, try this experiment. Draw two parallel lines, or stretch two strings 6 feet apart and 200 feet long. Then lope your horse between the lines. You will be amazed because very few show horses can do this. If you want to bet on it, your odds of winning money will be better in a Las Vegas casino.

So, we return once again to hindquarter control. The secret to straightness is hindquarter control, and this isn't a difficult maneuver to work on. The problem lies in omitting it during the training process. Trainers overlook forming the "straightness habit" and go on to bigger things, maneuvers that are more fun, not realizing that they may have missed the most important of the basics, and an element that would make those bigger things happen more easily for them.

If you think your horse travels straight, try this experiment. Draw two parallel lines, or stretch two ropes 6 feet apart and 200 feet long. Then lope your horse between the ropes. It's more difficult than you might think.

8 COLLECTION

> "Collection . . . is the state of the horse in which it relieves its forehand by increasing the load on the engaged hindquarters. . . . "

Given all of today's horse training styles, methods, and techniques, there is no area as widely misunderstood, nor as widely abused, as that generally referred to as "collection." Too often today's snaffle-bit pleasure classes and open pleasure classes are the perfect example of how the art of "bridling" a horse has disintegrated. (Bridling is defined as teaching a horse how to respond to the bit correctly, and to move with soft, supple collection in a bit.)

It's unbelievable to me that horses are allowed to win these classes displaying every mistake that is possible to make with the forward motion of a horse. Trainers spend hours teaching their horses to do things incorrectly, and they are firmly convinced that they are doing it correctly.

Knowledgeable judges are faced with the dilemma of finding a horse who even approaches correct bridle attitude, since all the horses in a class are often bridled in the same manner. As a result, judges are picking winners from an entire batch of falsely collected, movement-restricted horses.

Because of the recent attention given this subject by conscientious members of

The first attribute of a properly bridled horse is that he accept the bit and be comfortable with it, and not try to escape contact by lowering or raising his head, or by leaning on the bit. The second attribute is that the horse respond to the softest pull on the rein without attempting to evade it by tossing his head, opening his mouth, or any of the other ways that allow him to avoid it. This horse is listening and responding very softly when I simply pick up the bridle reins.

Here is an excellent example of a correctly collected horse working in balance. This is rider E. Dixon on Jubileaum, winner of the Grand Prix Special in the 1984 dressage competition at Devon, Pennsylvania.

the press, an awareness is beginning to develop. Nevertheless, I am firmly convinced that we have so far to go to rectify this situation that if we were to assemble one dozen of the world's greatest authorities on the art of bridling a horse (and they would probably be predominantly dressage people) to observe a western pleasure futurity or any major western pleasure event, they would be disgusted.

A natural question arises as to why this is, and how it has come to be the accepted style. I think one explanation is a link to misunderstood western tradition. Most western horses, especially those used in cow country, carry their heads naturally low (but seldom below the level of their withers), and are ridden on a loose rein. The early day cowboys were by no means reinsmen, but they did know that it was easier to rope a cow, cut one out of the herd, head one, or lope across a prairie-dog town when their mounts carried low heads.

Most of their horses were relaxed and carried their heads low for two reasons: first, the riders stayed off the horses' mouths; and, second, the horses were given lots of work. These horses weren't on 30-minute training sessions and then put back into a stall. They were ridden all day and the horses were happy to relax.

This attitude and tradition was naturally carried into the show ring and into western pleasure classes. Ask anyone who was judging western pleasure classes 30 years ago. The horses shown in those classes would still be all right, and they'd be a welcome improvement today because they at least represented a *natural* carriage. Their heads were not forced down, by use of gimmicks, into unnaturally low positions.

As time passed, however, the trainers exaggerated the situation; they wanted their horses' heads not only down, but also held in a vertical position, a kind of false collection. In order to achieve this, they have resorted to various kinds of gimmicks, sort of fast fixes, and these gimmicks translate into different forms of pure force.

One of the first gimmicks used is to run the bridle reins between a horse's front legs and up to the saddle horn, where they are tied. The horse's head is then locked down and the corners of his mouth (presuming the use of a snaffle bit, because a curb bit in this situation could really be devastating to a horse's

To begin teaching a horse how to correctly respond to the bit, softly take hold of him with light rein contact while the horse is standing still. At the slightest indication that he is trying to respond properly by dropping his chin, immediately release the contact. After doing this several times, and if he's beginning to readily respond, squeeze gently with both of your legs at the same time you apply soft pressure to the bit. This is the first step in achieving collection. **Photo by Peter Phinny**

methods to employ in the art of bridling a horse.

Therefore to begin our discussion of collection, we must first consider the attributes of a properly bridled horse. The first is that the horse accept the bit. He must be comfortable when in contact with the bit. A horse that constantly lowers his head is trying to escape contact. A horse should never abandon correct contact with a bit by getting above or behind it, or by leaning on it.

The second attribute is that the horse should respond to the softest pull on the reins without attempting to evade it by tossing his head, opening his mouth, or any of the ways that allow him to avoid giving us a softness in the mouth. When a horse accepts the bit and responds softly, he will be easy to collect.

Now, what is collection? In searching for a good definition, I once again return to Seunig's book *Horsemanship*. I think he described collection as well as anyone when he wrote: "Collection, as the term is used in dressage, is the state of the horse in which it relieves its forehand by increasing the load on the engaged hindquarters in order to concentrate all its forces for a given purpose. Carriage and responsiveness can be raised to their highest peaks, depending on the degree of collection."

Horsemen who understand the art of collecting a horse know that when the face of an *evenly balanced horse* approaches the vertical, there is an interplay of muscles down the horse's spinal column that will automatically lower and engage his hindquarters. In cowboy terms, "we put him on his back end." We all know that a horse can perform almost any maneuver best with engaged hindquarters. Running horses, barrel horses, reining horses, roping horses, all performance horses need to work off their back ends. Show me a horse who is heavy on the forehand, and I'll show you one who is awkward and sluggish.

Seunig, in describing collection, further writes: "In a correctly collected horse the croup and buttock muscles of the engaged hindquarters exert a powerful tug downwards and backwards upon the muscles of the back connected to them, thus lifting the chest and neck and taking some of the load off the forehand. The steps of the front end become loftier,

mouth) are bumped every time he moves a foreleg. There is nothing natural about a horse's movement in this situation.

Another device used is the draw rein. The principle remains the same; the only difference is that the trainer has fastened the horse's head slightly higher, and instead of alternately bumping his mouth on the corners, the horse's head is locked or fixed in place. In this position he is driven forward. Under these circumstances the horse cannot even be given the option of becoming acquainted with the give and take of a soft hand.

Another is the hock hobble. For this device, long reins to the bit are run through rings on each side of the saddle horn and down to rings fastened to a hobble buckled above and below each hock. Here again the horse has no way to avoid continuous, alternating pull on each side of his mouth.

Improperly adjusted hock hobbles used excessively will remove all feeling in a horse's mouth. This procedure is nothing more than a treatment in insensitivity, and these are not the correct

While walking the colt, I softly hold his face with light rein contact. If he slows down, I gently urge him forward with my legs, and ask again with a soft feel of the reins. If I succeed in getting him to break in his poll (flex) and to feel soft in my hands, even if for only a few steps, I relax my hands. After a few more steps, I apply soft rein contact again and ask him to "give me his face." Whenever I apply rein pressure, I also apply soft leg pressure to begin developing collection.

Photo by Peter Phinny

When the colt can walk completely around the pen bridled up, he will then be receptive to bridling up at the trot, and later at the lope.

Photo by Peter Phinny

1/ We all know that a horse can perform almost any maneuver best when his hindquarters are engaged, such as in a roll-back. This sequence on these two pages catches the colt just as he stops, and follows him as he drives out of the roll-back. This is the same colt that appears in the previous three photographs. Those were taken when he was a 2-year-old; these were taken a year later when he was 3.

2/

3/

4/

The initial work is best done in a snaffle bit because of the direct-rein action on the corners of the mouth.

Don't expect a horse to go immediately from a snaffle to a curb bit and to respond properly; he won't understand the pressure of the new bit. I feel that the best transitional bit is a Pelham with four reins. You can use the snaffle reins and at the same time slowly pull on the curb reins, gradually acquainting the horse with the feel of the curb chain.

their horses four-beat, or drag their hind legs. To point out an extreme, there are trainers who are now even filling their horse's hind shoes with lead in an effort to encourage hock engagement. This abuse is all done in the spirit of "horsemanship." Although this certainly points to a very distinct lack of understanding of the principles of collection, what a travesty for the poor horses.

Well, now it's time to learn to bridle our horse and teach him collection, to teach him without force or a tack room full of nonsense bits and gimmicks. The best way to approach the vertical with a horse's face is to softly take hold of him with the lightest rein contact (we, of course, begin with a mild snaffle bit), and this is best done while standing still.

If the horse evades by backing up, put him in a corner or with his rear end against a wall. When the horse attempts to drop his chin, immediately release the contact. Soon he will "face-up," but only for an instant. This is fine and it is all you want. Remember the Chinese proverb: "A journey of a thousand miles begins with a single step."

Keep your hands soft and ask your horse for only a little response. Build on what you get, and don't be afraid to wait for him to respond. Time doesn't mean anything. Let him think that it's his idea.

After several times of taking hold, feeling him soften, dwelling for an instant, and then releasing, also gently pressure him with both of your legs—a gentle squeeze. This is the first step in teaching him to engage his hindquarters. This should be a coordinated movement, a soft bit-contact and a soft, simultaneous squeeze. Always apply leg pressure as you hold his face.

Remember you are executing this at a standstill. When you are satisfied with your horse's response, dwell a little longer on the reins. Soon, at the mere hint of a tightened rein, his face will drop to the vertical. Depending on the individual horse, and your skill, it might only take a few sessions of this to get the results you want, or it might take longer. The important thing is not to ask for too

corresponding to the reduction of the load on the forehand."

In summing up the theory of collection, there are basic elements that are unmistakably evident. The first is that we cannot have a collected horse until his face approaches the vertical. Second, a horse's face cannot approach the vertical without his raising his chest and neck. Third, we get increased engagement of the hindquarters with a lowering of the croup, but not until the neck is raised.

If our pleasure horse trainers would only get this through their heads, their horses' lives would be infinitely more pleasant. Pulling a horse's head down below the wither level does not achieve any semblance of collection. This is further complicated when, in such a position, a horse's head is pulled to the vertical and sometimes even past the vertical. Talk about putting a horse on his front end! In this position the horse's topline becomes a complete arc and he looses all his hock engagement.

Some trainers can't figure out why

Horsemen who understand collection know that when a horse is evenly balanced, his face approaches the vertical and there is an interplay of muscles down the spinal column that will automatically lower and engage his hindquarters. This interplay of muscles is dramatically evident in this photograph of Rusty Dare, Hilliard, Ohio, stopping a reining horse.

Photo by Melissa M. Keehan

much; use the softest pull imaginable and wait for him to respond.

Don't be afraid to reissue the cues, and to wait. Wait. Wait. Wait. Softness is everything at this point; I believe that it is possible to collect a horse perfectly and never put over one-quarter of a pound of pull on the reins.

The initial work is best done in a snaffle bit because of the direct-rein action on the corners of the horse's mouth. While contacting the mouth, your hands should be on opposite sides of the saddle horn. It is advisable to conduct these training sessions on collection for only short periods of time. Nevertheless, these short sessions can be held several times during the course of an hour-long ride. In other words, don't spend the entire hour on collection only.

As it becomes easier for our colt to become collected, we can ask him to remain collected longer.

A horse does learn to collect through soft repetition; but on the other hand, don't overdo it because too much repetition will cause him to become bored. Vary your training and try to make it fun. To harp on the same movements in the same order destroys the horse's incentive.

We have now prepped our horse on the rudiments of collection at a standstill. When we begin to put him in motion, however, the same response will probably not come as easily. Again, the key is soft hands. We let our colt walk on a loose rein in a normal, relaxed walk. The walk is of fundamental importance; most trainers fail to school enough at this gait. If your horse can't perform at the walk, he sure can't at the trot or the lope when everything gets speeded up.

As we walk our colt, we again softly hold his face with slight rein/bit contact. He will probably slow down, but we gently urge him forward with our legs and ask again with a soft gathering of the reins. If we succeed in getting him to break in his poll and to feel soft in our hands, even if for only a few steps, this is fine; relax your hand, let him take a few more steps, and then establish contact and ask him again to collect. This is what I call "facing-up."

As our colt progresses, we can ask for his face for longer periods of time. As it becomes easier for him, we can ask him to remain collected longer. If we were to release each time he faced-up, he'd get the idea that we only wanted him to face-up for a few steps, and then he might become irritated when we ask for longer periods of collection. As we progress, the horse will indicate his reaction to the bridling process and we need to pay close attention to him. When he can walk completely around the pen bridled up, he will then be receptive to our rein action at the trot, and then at the lope.

For a bridle attitude at the trot, our cues are the same, and at the jog it's easy. At the lope, however, when the horse will very likely be inclined to push his nose out, his response to collection may come a little slower than we might think it should. Don't become impatient. Be careful to ask for only a few strides before you release him, and then ask again.

Be careful to collect him when he is at a relaxed lope, since this takes only a minimal pull. If the horse is high and loping in a tense, quick fashion, let him lope on a loose rein until he decides on his own to relax and slow down; then ask softly for collection.

In the mildest bit of them all, the snaffle, we have taught the rudiments of collection. We have him walking, trotting, and loping in a collected fashion while at the same time evidencing a relaxed and non-stressed attitude. He has learned to respond to the pressures of a snaffle on the corners of his mouth. Now, we are ready to leave the snaffle and move toward the curb bit, which is an entirely new situation.

The action of a curb bit at this stage is definitely strange. A horse feels the pressure of the curb strap or chain under his chin and his natural reaction is to move his head away from pressure, which in this case is up. We must, therefore, bridle our horse after the snaffle with some sort of transitional bit, one that slowly acquaints the horse with curb action. Don't ever expect a horse to go from the snaffle immediately into a curb and to understand the pressure of the new bit.

I feel that the best transitional bit is the Pelham with four reins. With this bit we can ride using the snaffle reins and, at the same time, slowly pull on the curb reins until the horse feels the curb chain. Remember the principle here: We are always trying to communicate with our horse. The Pelham, as a transitional bit between the snaffle-action and curb-

Here's a photo of a colt collected and bridled up nicely. Notice, too, that he is relaxed. Whenever a horse is feeling silly or high, let him lope on a loose rein until he decides to relax and slow down. Then ask softly for collection.

action bits, allows for a gradual communication of this new sensation the colt is feeling.

Let me recap. I feel that collection must be accomplished with hands, especially soft hands, and not with gimmicks. Anyone who has ridden a horse that is bridled correctly—one that responds by dropping his face nearly to the vertical on the mere lifting of the hand—knows what I am talking about. I don't want to force a horse to bridle up; I want him to do it on his own, but on my slightest cue.

I also want him to feel comfortable doing it. Don't ever forget the basics: soft hands. Reward him for each try. One step at a time. Wait for him. Perform correctly at the walk first. Constantly think, think, think. And finally, don't forget to watch him closely because he will tell you when he is ready to proceed to the next stage of his schooling. The process of teaching collection takes time, so don't try to rush it.

Believe me, this old adage applies: "A good start is half the finish." Establish good collection and you will be building a foundation upon which to develop a finished horse.

73

9 LATERAL CONTROL

Lateral control is essential in making a top performance horse.

A spin is an advanced lateral movement built with a solid foundation. We can achieve a finished maneuver, such as Kim is demonstrating here, if at every increase of speed we know where each foot is when it's ready to move. This is timing, and timing is so important. At this instant, the mare's outside hind leg (right) is propelling her into the spin. With the next step, the inside pivot foot will be locked down.

After we have mastered calmness, have our horse evenly loaded and going straight, and after we are able to collect him softly and at any gait, we are ready for lateral control.

Any change in direction involves laterals—lateral movement. How we handle lateral control, however, is paramount to our success in making a top horse. Smooth lateral maneuvers are keyed to hindquarter control, and when we address hindquarter control we are focusing on the use of the rider's leg. Of course, the rider's hands and seat are

To teach a horse to move his hindquarters away from leg pressure, we begin with an exercise known as a pass around the forehand, or turn on the forehand. Here, Kim is moving the colt's hindquarters to the left, passing them around his right foreleg. She has shortened her right rein, and is gently bumping the horse with her right leg. Although we can't see it, her left leg is away from the horse so it's not applying pressure or feel.

important in all phases of horsemanship, but in the case of laterals, the rider's leg is the predominant schooling aid. The rider's leg not only puts the horse in motion, it also maintains that motion. This is an important consideration.

A rider can pressure with his leg or bump with it, depending on what cue is needed. He can even reprimand with his leg if that is needed. The rider can position his leg against the horse's side so as to either hold the horse's position, or to move his hindquarters laterally. If pressured with both legs simultaneously, the horse moves forward, or speeds up if he is already in motion. The legs are the rider's driving force and his skillful use of them has much to do with determining the success of his training program. It may surprise some, but I believe a rider's legs are more important than his hands in properly controlling a horse.

An important point to remember is that the improper use of one's legs can result in circumstances as disastrous as the improper use of one's hands. Many riders bang or tap their horses with their legs, or swing their legs forward and back. Sometimes these actions become unconscious habits and the horse gradually loses sensitivity to leg pressure.

These same riders can't figure out why they have no leg control, which the horse so desperately needs, especially when he is in motion.

Before getting into the how-to of lateral control, I want to define "inside" and "outside." Whenever the horse is moving to the right, his right side is the inside, and his left side is the outside. When traveling to the left, his left side is the inside and his right side, the outside.

In order to acquaint the horse with our leg, to teach him to move his hindquarters away from our leg pressure and to obey our leg, we can employ a series of exercises which surely work. These exercises have been in use for at least a thousand years, so they are not new or startling.

The first is a pass around the forehand, also known as a turn on the forehand. Let's assume we want to pass him around his right foreleg. This means his right foreleg should stay in place, and that his hindquarters will be going to the left. We shorten our right rein, and pressure the horse with our right leg behind the cinch. All we want is a step or two. Our left rein is reasonably loose unless we need it to stop forward motion.

If the horse takes a step or two with

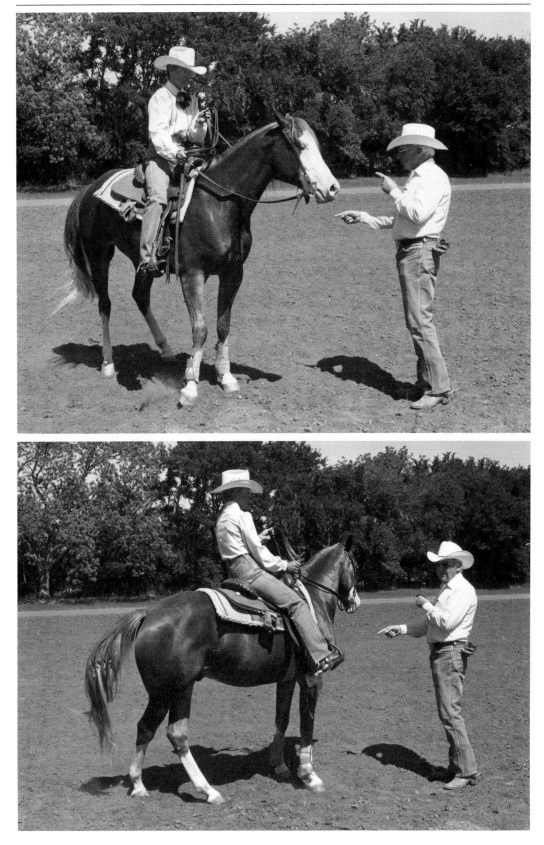

To pass around the colt's left foreleg, Kim shortens her left rein and applies pressure with her left leg, while keeping her right leg away from the colt.

his hindquarters in the correct direction, relax the cue, wait, and then cue him again. Don't expect him to understand the entire concept immediately, but in a relatively short period of time he'll take a series of steps, and after a few sessions he'll make a full 360-degree turn around the forehand.

Remember to work both sides of the horse equally. To make a pass around his left foreleg, shorten your left rein, and apply pressure with your left leg to move the hindquarters to the right. When the horse understands what we're after and becomes accustomed to this movement, he will step his hindquarters the full 360 degrees with only slight leg pressure.

Another exercise that now becomes easy is the two-track. In this case we ask for hindquarter control while in motion. Walk the horse in a straight line along the fence and ask him to move his hindquarters to the inside (center of arena), while keeping his head and neck straight ahead. The horse's back legs will move in a different set of tracks than his front legs, hence the name two-tracks.

To execute this movement as a correct dressage maneuver requires more body alignment, collection, and finesse than we in the western world commonly give it. For our purposes we are satisfied with the horse's simple two-track movement rather than the specific movement as defined by dressage riders.

After the horse learns the two-track, a side-pass can be easily introduced. One simple approach is to face a wall or a fence, and to tap or bump with the left leg until we get a few crossover side steps to the right, or vice-versa. The fence serves to keep the horse from wanting to go forward.

Hold the outside rein steady, and slightly open up the inside rein (the rein in the direction you are attempting to move). As you cue with your outside leg, he will begin to understand this move sideways and will cross his legs as he moves. Don't hurry him, let him understand what you're asking. Soon the side steps become easy and the horse can

While this horse is moving forward, Kim asks him to move his hindquarters to the right, by shortening her left rein and bumping with her leg behind the cinch.

perform them without the aid of a fence.

The single most important principle to remember here is that hindquarter control determines the effectiveness of overall control. Many trainers forget hindquarter control and constantly focus on the head and neck since they are convinced that the neck is the steering wheel. These riders grab hold of the steering wheel as quickly as possible and are determined to control the horse from the front end, from front to rear.

The exact opposite is what I'm proposing here; you communicate integral control best from the rear end, rear to front. We work on the hindquarters to achieve good results with the neck.

With a proficiency in these basic maneuvers, we are ready for actual work on laterals. These controls fall into two categories. In the first category we use our inside leg and outside rein, or vice-versa. This is called diagonal control. In the second category we use the inside rein and the inside leg. This is called lateral control.

Here's an example of a mare in the beginning stages of a two-track. While the mare is moving forward alongside the fence, Kim applies pressure with her left leg to move the hindquarters to the right, so they move in a different set of tracks. This is another phase of developing hindquarter control.

To become proficient in applying diagonal and lateral control, there is one basic, all-important rule: *Know where the horse's feet are.* Know the location of his front feet while he is in motion, and his rear feet as well.

To know, however, requires one vital capacity: concentration. A rider must continually think, feel, and visualize the position of each foot during the sequence of the horse's stride. Ray Hunt is an absolute master in this area, and as a result he can do unbelievable things with his horses, even green horses. He preaches to his students: "Pick up his right front foot, move his left hind foot," etc.

He was the first person I know of who worked his students on counting cadence on a given footfall. He teaches them to realize how important it is to know where the horse's feet are. He puts on the most impressive demonstration I have seen on foot placement and control. He stands his horse quietly on all four feet, and then moves any one of his horse's feet, in any direction, independent of the other feet. A back foot forwards, inside,

outside, wherever, with all the other feet grounded. He does this without visible cues. This is control.

Knowing where a horse's feet are makes them easier to direct when we put them in motion, and this is what lateral control is all about. One of the first exercises I teach my colts is a 180-degree turn over the hocks—a roll-back so to speak, at the walk. Knowing where a colt's feet are is so much easier at the walk than at the trot or the lope.

All of these 180-degree turns which we execute are predetermined, and at first we begin slowly along a fence. We want our colt to stop, to walk his front end *toward* the fence and therefore around his inside hind foot (keeping his body straight), and then to walk off in the opposite direction. This maneuver will teach a young horse hock engagement and position him to lower his croup as he makes the turn. We are encouraging him to use his back end. The fence is an aid because it serves to keep the horse from making a "bicycle turn" or a U-turn.

Two photos of Kim showing how she uses a fence to teach the side-pass to a colt. The fence stops the colt's forward motion and encourages him to move laterally. Because Kim is asking the colt to side-pass to her left, she is applying pressure from her right leg.

Once a horse becomes proficient in side-passing, he can do it in the open, as Kim demonstrates in these two photos. She is side-passing to her right. Note how the colt is crossing his left front leg over the right front (above), and his left hind over the right hind (below). Also note how Kim is handling the reins.

To teach a colt a 180-degree turn over his hocks, we begin by stopping him and walking his front end around his inside hind foot (left foot in this picture), and toward the fence. We keep his body straight, and then walk off in the opposite direction.

When the colt begins making nice turns without forward motion (they are so fluid feeling that you'll definitely know), then we turn him *away* from the fence so that he does not become dependent on it. At the next stage, we make all turns in the middle of the arena away from all fences.

Our cues for the 180-degree turn over the hocks are simple. Let's assume that we are walking along a fence which is on our right. We stop our horse with a slight pull on the left rein. This grounds the left foot. We then softly lift our right rein with an easy backward pull. The colt moves his right forefoot (the inside one) laterally and back. This is the beginning of his turn, and almost simultaneously we pressure him with our outside leg. This action holds his rear end in place and provides impulse for the next step as he completes this walk around his inside hind foot. This is a surprisingly simple movement that the colt soon finds easy.

An important element connected to the success of this lesson is to concentrate on picking up the inside forefoot first. This foot needs to be the first one to move, and it becomes easier for the colt to handle after he tries it a few times. Don't forget that anytime you move the horse's front end laterally, the inside foot leaves the ground first. Pay attention to this element in the maneuver.

Everything involved in the training of a horse is interconnected; if we have done a good job schooling for the pass around the forehand, this roll-back at the walk becomes simple. The secret of a correct lateral move remains hindquarter control. The front end only initiates the turning, the back end powers it.

81

1/

2/

You work to communicate where you want him to move his foot.

On the 180-degree turn, the horse should keep his body alignment nearly straight. This is done with your outside leg and rein. As you pick the inside forefoot off the ground, make sure that you don't pull hard enough to force the colt to give with his neck only. The rider's outside leg maintains the straightness and provides impulse for the turn.

Think about how the horse is balanced in this instance. His center of gravity lies behind a diagonal line joining the outside forefoot with the inside hindfoot. We are not only lifting the forefoot, we are directing it as well.

When we put the horse in faster motion, we can further direct him laterally (if our timing is accurate) by doing just what we've been practicing: by picking up the inside forefoot as it comes off the

ground. This simple movement really produces results, but it requires timing. As his inside forefoot leaves the ground, a slight pull directs the leg to the inside.

You work to communicate where you want him to move his foot. This also happens to be, at a later stage, the best way to keep a horse from bearing out in a circle. You must concentrate on where his feet are, and then your outside leg will keep him straight.

Most trainers power their horses into a lateral movement with a strong neck rein or hard inside pull. If you have pretty much trained this way, and you want to see things get easier quickly, work on picking up the inside front foot as it leaves the ground, and know where your horse's feet are.

Here's a sequence of five photos showing a roll-back. The secret of a correct lateral move like this is hindquarter control. The hindquarters power the roll-back; the front end only initiates the turning. On a 180-degree turn like a roll-back, the horse should keep his body alignment nearly straight. The rider does this by using the outside rein and leg (left in this case). The outside cues not only help maintain straightness, but also provide impulse for the turn.

Spins, roll-backs, and circles are all lateral movements built through a solid foundation, and in all of them the inside forefoot must leave the ground first. We can achieve these finished maneuvers if we always know where each foot is when it is ready to move. We cannot do anything with a foot when it is on the ground or when it is in the air, but we can direct it as it leaves the ground. This is timing, and this timing is so important.

Again, I can't repeat this enough: watch your horse; by his reactions he will tell you how well he understands your communication.

A rider must always know where the horse's feet are in applying lateral and diagonal control. Ray Hunt is an absolute master at being able to place his horse's feet where he wants them, and I love to practice it, as I'm doing here. This photo was taken when this colt was a 2-year-old. Those on the next three pages were taken in the summer of his 3-year-old year.

Photo by Peter Phinny

1/ A series of six pictures in which Kim is schooling a 3-year-old in a spin, which requires lateral control. Here, the colt is crossing over nicely, and has his pivot foot (right hind) planted nicely.

2/ The colt is about ready to pick up his left front and cross it over his right front.

3/ Kim keeps her weight squarely in the middle of the colt's back, and keeps her inside (right) leg away from his side.

4/ The colt keeps his pivot foot planted as he comes around. Notice how relaxed he is, even though he is turning with some speed, as evidenced by his tail and the reins.

5/ Although this picture is a little blurry, you can see how he is picking up his inside front foot to move it over.

6/ Kim keeps pressuring lightly with her outside foot as the colt keeps turning. Remember: The front end initiates the turning, while the hindquarters power it.

10 LEAD CHANGES

The preparation for the lead change is the rider's responsibility.

Throughout the gamut of western training, probably no subject is as controversial or as seemingly mysterious as that of leads and lead changing. Nearly all trainers feel they have mastered the art of lead changing. However, if we were to ask 100 trainers how to change leads, we might very well get 100 different answers.

Although most horsemen can recognize a change, I suppose that 90 percent of them really don't understand what takes place during the change, let alone how to make the preparatory moves to facilitate a clean change of leads. Even though it is the rider's responsibility to

prepare the horse to execute a lead change, unfortunately the horse will take the blame if he misses the change.

Often when selecting their prospects—and reining futurity prospects serve as a classic example—trainers demand a colt that makes clean lead changes even in the pasture. If they find a semi-broke prospect, the first thing that they try is the lead change. All are looking for a natural lead changer. I don't think that this is all bad because a natural lead changer is, more often than not, a pretty coordinated pony. But all horses will miss lead changes on occasion and, as a rule, the preparation for the lead change

When the inside fore-leg or leading leg (left in this picture) pushes off during a lope, a period of suspension follows. It is during this moment when the hind legs can switch their functions. If we can hold the inside (leading) hind leg for an instant when it hits the ground, the outside hind leg (right in this photo) would then be allowed the freedom and time to move forward, making the lead change behind. Almost simultaneously, the horse would also change leads in front.

To have any success teaching lead changes, you must have an absolutely quiet pupil. Calmness is everything. Notice how quiet this buckskin is as he reaches that moment of suspension when the lead change can take place.

is the rider's responsibility.

To begin, however, we need a definition. A lead change is a phase sequence in forward motion when the hind legs and then the front legs interchange their roles. If the horse had been traveling on the left lead, he's now on the right lead. If we actually study the legs in motion, we can understand what happens.

When the inside fore, or lead leg, pushes off in the lope, a period of suspension follows; it is during this moment when the hind legs can switch their functions. If we can hold the inside hind leg for an instant when it hits the ground, the outside hind leg is then allowed the freedom and time to move forward. This interchanges the role of the hind legs and completes the lead change. Almost simultaneously what had previously been the outside forefoot strikes the ground, and is now the inside forefoot in the new direction.

Before we decide how to execute and cue for this desired change, let's talk dos and don'ts and things in general about lead changes.

The first rule of major importance: Do not drill, school, practice, or force lead changes on your horse. Nothing will get you in trouble more quickly than

To teach the canter departure, stand your horse squarely at the end of the arena or training area, away from the fences. Here, I'm going to ask for a right canter departure, so I'm squeezing with my left leg behind the cinch and am slightly lifting the left rein. My right leg is sort of pointing the lead I want him to take.

1/ In this series of six photos, Kim lets the filly trot into the canter departure. This is okay. If Kim is quiet with her, before long she'll confidently pick up the lope when the cues are issued. Kim is asking the filly for the right lead; therefore, she is squeezing with her left leg behind the cinch, and pointing with her right foot. Notice how Kim also keeps the filly's body straight, which is very important.

In the early stages, it sometimes helps to exaggerate the cues. This doesn't mean to use force; just to use a little body English and leg pressure to communicate the cues more effectively the first few times.

2/

3/

4/

5/

6/

this. The only time to school for this movement is after the horse has had lots of preliminary work and is fully prepared for it. If you make work on lead changes uncomfortable for your horse, you will regret your actions.

The second rule: To have any success teaching lead changes, you must have an absolutely quiet pupil. Calmness is everything. A tense horse pays little attention to the finely timed and positioned cues necessary to complete the change. So, keep your horse quiet. Nervous horses tend to rush through their lead changes and they won't keep their bodies straight; they don't respond to our aids. Ray Hunt has a good adage that applies here: "If you don't have his attention, don't try to direct it."

The third rule: There is no other schooling maneuver that a horse learns to anticipate as quickly as a lead change. If we drill or over-school or attempt lead changes before the horse is ready, his anticipation will destroy our progress. When a horse anticipates, he knows what is coming and attempts to do it on his own prematurely, and invariably he will do it wrong.

The strange thing about his anticipation is that no matter how careful we are not to pre-convey our cues, the horse knows what is coming. All one needs to do is *think* lead change and the horse will become a mind reader. It is uncanny, but true.

The fourth rule: Never whip or spur a horse when he is making a change. If the horse knows that the change is coming, and if he also knows the spur comes with it, he will rush through his change, and before long he'll be running away at the slightest suggestion of a lead change.

An element linked to this rule involves changing leads by speeding the horse up. It is easier for a horse to change cleanly when he is running fast. Why? Because the period of suspension lasts longer at speed, which gives the horse more time to interchange the hind legs. However, the successful results are short-lived. Don't try changing at speed unless you are prepared for an eventual run-off.

Sometimes I see quiet reining horses that have been previously shown for a season or two get into the hands of a beginner, or a non-pro, and develop problems in their circles. Most likely the horse has begun to bear out in his circles, and when it comes time for a lead change, the "wreck" is on. Why does this happen? Because the horse was not schooled properly in his early training—he was not taught to change leads slowly and calmly.

What does the owner do when this happens? Invariably he takes the horse to a trainer for help, and the trainer is forced into a quick-fix situation. So he snatches the horse when he rushes. He is working on the problem, not on the cause of it; as a result, the horse rarely remains fixed. Remember: For any lasting solution, remove the cause in order to effect the cure.

All right, it is now time for the specifics. How do we teach a horse to change leads, and not just change but do it softly, calmly, and on any given stride? The first consideration: Lead changing is completely a matter of hindquarter control, and the lead change can't be successful without it. Since a change is a hind-leg switch, you must have control of his hindquarters; it's that clear-cut. If you have your doubts, try making changes with the front end first.

So, the first requirement is a flawless canter departure. When your horse does a perfect canter departure with his body straight, your lead changes will come. The canter departure that we're after occurs when we can apply a leg cue at the standstill, feel the horse position his body, and then lope off without even one trotting step. Here's how I like to work towards this goal.

There is no other schooling maneuver that a horse learns to anticipate as quickly as a lead change.

1/ Kim demonstrates a drop-to-the-trot change of leads in this sequence of five photos. She starts out by loping halfway down the working area in the right lead.

Stand your horse squarely at the end of the arena or training area and away from the fences. To ask for a left-lead canter departure, squeeze with your right leg behind the cinch, and slightly lift the leading (left) rein, then trot him into a lope. Don't be too demanding. If he takes the wrong lead, do not snatch back on the bridle reins or punish him. Let him lope to the other end quietly in the wrong lead. Turn him around and ask again.

Don't expect perfection immediately. Don't punish him if he misses. Reissue the cues and try again, and always cue your horse quietly and softly. If you try constantly to make corrections, you will confuse your horse. Make sure that you cue exactly the same way each time. Don't force it on him, let him find it. There is a big difference. If you let your horse discover for himself what you are suggesting, he'll remember it and he'll execute it without stress.

Also, do not alternate cues each time you reach the end of the training area. I think it's best to school in one lead until he is pretty comfortable with it and will canter depart correctly eight times out of ten. When he's proficient in one lead, then school in the other lead until he is equally proficient in it. You can start alternating when the horse is accustomed to both canter departures.

The secret is to keep him quiet. If you have trouble, always go back to the pass around the forehand to sharpen him up for the canter departures. Remember: We are concentrating on hindquarter control; we're building a solid foundation which our horse understands and with which he feels comfortable.

Always work to keep your horse's body straight during the departures. Lope straight lines each time you depart.

During your canter departures, always move your leg forward on the lead side. In other words, when you squeeze

2/ She checks him softly . . .

3/ . . . just enough to break him down to a trot.

4/ Then she immediately applies the cues for the left lead.

5/ As the colt picks it up, she collects him again and continues loping in a straight line.

with your outside leg behind the cinch, move your inside leg forward. You sort of point with your inside foot the lead you want him to take.

Let's assume you now have your horse departing correctly from a standstill every time, without having to trot first, and are loping back and forth across the training area on a straight line. Now it's time for a lead change. Lope him halfway across the training area and check him softly, just enough to slow him to a trot. As soon as he breaks stride, issue your cues to leg him off on the opposite lead. When you leg him off, make certain to move your leg forward on the new lead side. This drop-to-the-trot change is also called a simple change.

When you check him from the lope, work to make the trotting steps fewer and fewer until you do only two before the new lead departure. Keep doing this and your horse will get better each day. Soon the simple lead change will get to be an easy routine for him and he'll develop an attitude like, "This is kindergarten, I want to go to high school." Have confidence that the lead changes will come, and just keep everything cool, calm, and collected.

When it becomes really easy for your horse and the check requires only one trotting stride before he takes the new lead, you are ready to proceed.

Okay, you are loping toward the middle of the pen on a straight line. As his leading forefoot strikes the ground, squeeze with your leg on the same side and move your other leg forward in a simultaneous motion. For example, if you are loping on the left lead, squeeze with your left leg and move your right leg forward—to change him to the right lead.

The horse should make the change. If he doesn't, try again. Remember: *Your cue is issued when the lead forefoot strikes the ground.* His first change will most likely be sort of an awkward hop, but you will know it. The first change is a thrill for most riders; it is what we have worked for and it is a triumph of sorts. There is no end to the satisfaction

a rider gets experiencing his first correctly cued lead change.

The horse may be a little more proficient on one side than on the other, but this is okay. He will even out in time. After he begins making his changes fairly easily, he may come to a stage when he will execute his changes on his own—uncalled-for changes. Don't worry about this as it is actually a blessing in disguise. He has learned how to make changes off your leg and in straight lines, and this is what you want. He's demonstrating a willingness to please, and soon he will make changes on any stride you ask for.

Yes, I know I said earlier that we do not want the horse to anticipate his lead changes. But remember: We are not working in figure-eights, and this is not an old war horse anticipating changes. This is a colt trying to figure out how to please us. Reprimanding him at this early stage could destroy the calm attitude we have worked to develop.

It will become easier and easier to make changes, but remember these things: Keep his body straight, make sure that you have hindquarter control, and that he responds to your leg aids. When he has reached this stage, don't practice drop-to-the-trot changes; that is a step backwards and he has moved up a grade. Of course, you still need patience, but once he understands how to change off your leg, we don't need to reinforce the easier drop-change.

Many of us have observed horses competing in western riding classes at horse shows. This is a beautiful class and we see horses that are thoroughly schooled in the art of changing leads. If you are a student of these horses, you are aware that it is the calm horse that always wins. The lead changes demonstrated by the winning horses are precise, simultaneous, and in perfect stride. This is what we are after, and I honestly

Your cue is issued when the lead forefoot strikes the ground.

1/ Here's a terrific sequence of four pictures showing Kim making a flying change of leads. She's loping on the right lead, and as soon as his leading forefoot strikes the ground . . .

feel that even uncoordinated horses can be taught to change cleanly. With this type of horse, we must spend more time on hindquarter control and probably wait longer for the horse to get it all together. However, the cues and the procedures remain the same.

The movements linked to the lead-changing maneuver, like so many of the others, are merely progressions of body-control movements using our legs to direct the hindquarters.

Remember: Don't try to force lead changes on your horse—let them happen, let him find them. Keep your horse calm and quiet; patience is everything. Recognize and reward him when he tries; and again, observe him closely and he'll tell you how well you're getting your ideas across.

2/ . . . she squeezes with her right leg to ask for the left lead. The outside hind leg (left) has already moved forward to become the leading leg behind, and the outside front leg is just a fraction of a second behind in changing.

3/ As the forefeet come down, the left leg is now the leading leg.

4/ Kim continues loping in the left lead in a straight line.

11 STOPS

If a horse has been taught to respond to cues, to engage his hindquarters correctly, and to approach the stop with straightness and balance, he can stop calves or slide in a reining pattern.

Here's a great example of the slide necessary to win in today's reining competition. This is Kim Diercks riding Papa Jess, owned by Peter Phinny, at the 1988 NRHA Futurity. This gelding is the same buckskin pictured at various stages of training in other chapters in this book.

Photo by Waltenberry

When the primary use of a western horse is ranch work, there is really only one objective as far as the stop is concerned, and that is to train your horse to drive his hindquarters into the ground in order to abruptly halt. To a rancher, stopping doesn't mean sliding 30 feet while the horse's front feet lightly walk across perfectly manicured arena ground. To a rancher, stopping means quickly coming to a halt to control a calf on the end of his rope or to turn in the opposite direction to head off a cow.

What we have seen over the past 30 or so years is the evolution of certain styles in some of the western performance events. Whether these styles are good or bad is subject to debate. The reining horse's sliding stop is a perfect example of this evolution. This style of stop definitely shows off a horse's athletic ability and separates average horses from the very best. It is, in a sense, an element of sport rather than a representation of function as it once was. I don't think this is bad; it's simply the way the sport has developed.

I also believe that for schooling pur-

This is another terrific example of the type of stop it takes to win in today's high-caliber reining competition. This is Mr Melody Jac, ridden by Tim McQuay to win the 1988 NRHA Futurity, and owned by Otto Schubert of Smithtown, New York. This is also a great example of how a horse's hindquarters will almost drop out from under the rear saddle skirts when he uses his loin properly in a stop.

Photo by Waltenberry

poses the principles of a good stop transcend style. If a horse has been taught to respond to cues, to engage his hindquarters correctly, and to approach the stop with straightness and balance, he can stop calves or slide in a reining pattern.

I do acknowledge that there are hollow-back sliding stops, sort of trick stops, that, unfortunately, can get by in a reining pattern, but that would be ridiculous in a roping arena or on a ranch. We won't concern ourselves with them. We will address the subject of teaching a horse to stop in the same way that we have approached the other topic areas,

as a part of our interconnected program.

Nothing is inconsistent with what has been established in the earlier chapters; a true stop is another rung on the ladder. So, whether you're interested in teaching your horse a sliding stop or a working horse stop, please pay attention to the basic movements. We will discuss at some length the conditions necessary for a sliding stop, and for teaching a horse to slide. But bear in mind that what we're discussing is not unrelated to a roping horse stop; it is simply a stylized version of a basic stop.

101

This picture of Joe Beaver roping at the 1987 National Finals Rodeo illustrates the typical hard stop of a calf-roping horse. The horse uses his hindquarters in much the same way as in a slide, but because he is being asked to stop quickly, he uses his front end to help in the stop. In a sliding stop, the horse is cued and conditioned to keep his front end loose and moving in a balanced trotting action.
Photo by James Fain

There is no reason why a horse that has been taught to stop and to slide properly can't be prepared to stop abruptly and to work a calf; this is actually a function of changing the shoes used on his hind feet and communicating the purpose of an abrupt stop by introducing the horse to working conditions.

In an abrupt stop, the horse uses his hindquarters in much the same way as in a slide, but because he is being asked to stop quickly, he uses his front end to help in the stop. In a sliding stop, the horse is cued and conditioned to keep his front end loose and moving in a balanced trotting action.

In regard to a stylized stop, probably there is no more spectacular sight, at any horse event, than a slide 40 feet long.

The horse is running wide open and with the flick of the rider's finger, the horse drops his rear end, engages his hocks, and trots with his front feet as he slides. This can be a beautiful maneuver, but how do we get it?

First of all, stops aren't really all that difficult; they are part of a progression beginning with a simple halt at the walk and the trot, and the horse must be positioned for them and not forced into them. Many trainers make use of fences and walls to stop their horses; others stop with a direct pull in the open (away from a fence). We see great sliding horses all performing exceedingly well and yet each has been trained in a different manner. Nevertheless, there are two considerations that everyone seems to agree

A cutter does not want his horse to slide. He wants him to lock down immediately, as Quixotes Shey has done here, in order to stay in control of the cow. The rider is John Starrak of Edgefield, South Carolina. **Photo Courtesy of NCHA**

on: good ground and the correct shoes.

To slide well, a horse must be on a good sliding surface. Just as you cannot ski without snow, you must have good ground to school for sliding stops. What is good ground? It is a firm, smooth base with a thick layer of sand on top approximately two inches thick.

A horse soon becomes accustomed to a stopping surface; he definitely will not slide on just any kind of footing, especially during the initial training period. Therefore, it's important to school on a surface familiar to him until he is sliding pretty well.

The surface or ground also requires constant care. Because sliding ground is most likely sand over a firm base, it is important to harrow or drag the sand to maintain a uniform consistency. This also takes care of any minor ruts, holes, or depressions.

The second important factor in teaching the slide is the hind shoes. A good farrier is a must, and shoeing a sliding horse is an art form in its own right. To shoe a horse properly, a good farrier studies the structure of the hip, leg, hock, and foot. In many instances a farrier will shoe a horse several times before finding the right combination of angles and shoes. This is particularly true on horses with conformational problems.

Rear shoes on reiners are called sliders and come in a variety of sizes and styles. Their width varies from ¾ to 1¼ inches. Most, however, are in the 1-inch range.

After shoeing a horse for the first time with sliders, do not attempt to stop him for several days. Let him get acquainted with the shoes because they are somewhat slippery, and the horse must learn

1/ This is a series of four pictures showing Kim asking a 3-year-old colt to stop from the trot. Here, she's moving at a nice trot.

2/ She's taken the slack out of the reins and is holding them softly while leaning back slightly.

3/ She sits deep in the saddle and . . .

4/ . . . waits for him to stop. She let him find the stop; she didn't jerk or pressure him into it.

1/ Here's another series of four pictures showing Kim stopping the colt from a lope. She's loping quietly at a moderate speed.

2/ Kim has asked him to stop by saying whoa, taking the slack out of the reins, sitting deep, and leaning back.

3/ The colt momentarily stiffens his poll and jaw and pops Kim up, but . . .

4/ . . . immediately softens, drops his hindquarters, and makes a nice stop.

If the horse doesn't slide (and this one isn't) when you ask him, pay him no attention and, above all, don't get mad. Instead, gather him into a complete stop, which might take several strides, sit on him for at least 30 seconds, then turn around and lope off.

to balance on them. It is almost like putting on skates for the first time. Let the horse figure them out, and make certain that you only stop from the trot for the first few weeks.

All right. When we have good ground and our horse is shod properly, where do we start? Again, slides are part of a progression, and we start at the beginning. If the horse can't stop at the walk and the trot, he surely can't stop correctly when running wide open.

It is best to walk around the pen, take the slack out of the reins, say "whoa" (a voice command for the horse's benefit), and sit deeply in the saddle with a backwards motion of your upper body. We exaggerate our body position—leaning back—at first to help the horse learn the meaning in our weight shift. Eventually, very slight movements will help signal our cues. Let the horse stand quietly for a moment and then do it again.

If he refused to stand quietly, back him for one step and then release the reins. When you ask him to halt, let him find what it is that you want; don't back-pressure with your reins and force him down. He needs to think through this. Our first stops at the walk need not be on stopping ground.

After a few tries at the walk, we should feel the horse lower his hindquarters as we pick up on the reins. We only *pick up* on the reins, we don't pull.

When he stops and stands quietly at the walk, repeat the exercise at the slow jog. All we are after here is a halt and to stand quietly.

Each time we ask for a stop, remember our body cues; sit deeply and lean back. Use only the lightest pull. Don't demand perfection; just say whoa, pick up on the reins softly, and wait.

Because of all the time we have spent on him up to this point, he understands

Then try it again, and you'll probably have better luck, as Kim is having here. The point is that we are trying to set up a situation in which the horse enjoys taking part. He should not feel hurried, forced, or pressured, and he should be able to relax afterwards. If we can constantly convey this to him, he will catch on and begin to understand what is coming and prepare for it. When this happens, we are definitely making progress.

collection; therefore, when we pick up on the reins, he knows that we are asking him to break at the poll and to collect himself.

There is one cardinal rule in regard to sliding: Never pull, snatch, or jerk on your horse. Hint with the reins, and do the rest with your seat and upper body. Ask, do not demand, and do not practice stops for long periods of time. Ask for one or two and then go do something else.

When you feel the horse begin to drop his rear end at the jog, you can ask for a little more, and a little more means increasing the pace to a trot. The cues are the same; you want to feel his rear end dropping. Always let him stand for a few seconds before trotting him off again. This is a reward.

If at first the horse tries to move forward after a stop, I like to back him for a step or two. Other trainers turn their horses around after the stop and trot off in a different direction. This effectively discourages the horse from moving forward after the stop.

At the trot we will begin to see short slide marks of about two or three feet on the ground. We can build on this.

When we move to the extended trot, the important thing to remember is to make doubly sure the horse's body is straight when we issue our cues. If the horse has constantly been stopped with his body straight, he soon thinks that this is the only way he can stop, and this is a decided advantage when we ask for more speed.

Remember: Straightness means even loading. If a horse's weight is evenly loaded on all four quarters, we get less evasion and straighter stops.

Again, a word of warning: Do not ask for many stops in sequence, just one or two and then go do something else.

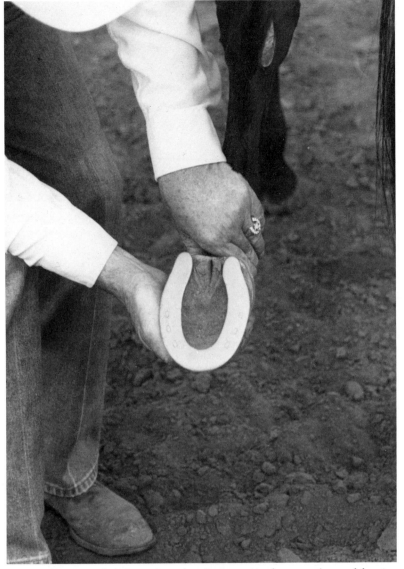

Here's the type of sliding shoe that I use on my horses. A good farrier plays a key role in shoeing a horse to allow him to slide to the best of his ability.

learned to use his front end, and we haven't had enough speed to warrant it.

Head position is important and, provided the horse has been schooled properly on collection and in the basics, we should be able to softly hold him without his head flying out of position. If he tends to nose out, don't worry. If you try to demand too much "face" or flexion during the slide, it can upset his natural balance and he'll tend to prop himself on his front feet. The horse's head and neck are his balancing mechanism during the slide, and it is best not to try serious adjustments here.

Unless his head gets completely out of control, be content with his basic recognition of your desire for him to collect himself. He will tell you where his head is most comfortable, and you will feel his collection. To demand too much positioning of his head could throw his balance off significantly and result in a very awkward stop.

If his head should become uncontrolled and inadvertently cause him to be out of balance in a slide, use your hands more to communicate a better head position until he feels comfortable. This is simply a process of giving him confidence and steadying him; it is not a time to jerk on him or to resort to any mechanical devices.

It is important that the horse use his loin during any stop and particularly during the slide. When he flexes his loin, his entire rear quarters have tremendous engagement, as evidenced by an almost sit-down position. In this position a horse can hold his balance over the ground and we won't see skip-slides or one-foot slides.

When a horse uses his loin, his back end almost drops out from under the rear skirts of the saddle. This is where the term "melts into the ground" takes on meaning, and this is one of the reasons why most horsemen, from the standpoint of conformation, are partial to strong-loined horses.

When our horse handles the stop from the extended trot, when he collects himself and remains straight and balanced on our soft cues, we're ready to advance

If you drill on stops, you are asking for trouble.

As the horse progresses to the extended trot, the slide marks will begin to tell the tale. We will be seeing marks 6 to 10 feet long. At this point, our horse is balancing himself correctly during the slides, and he is beginning to feel for the ground.

From the extended trot, our slide should involve little more than lifting of the hands and a shifting of our weight by leaning back slightly. The slightest pull should drop his rear end and engage his hocks. At this stage, he has not

This horse, Lisa Dry Boss, ridden by Matt Lantz, also exemplifies the present reining-horse stop. Notice how quiet and relaxed the horse is while sliding behind and trotting in front. Over the past 20 or so years, certain styles have evolved in some of the western performance events, and the reining horse's slide is a perfect example of this evolution.

Photo by Harold Campton

We are trying to set up a situation in which the horse enjoys stopping.

Always keep your horse straight when making a run-down prior to a stop.

to the lope. When beginning this phase, make sure that the horse is loping calmly and on a loose rein. If we try to stop him when he is charging, it requires a strong pull and he will not be mentally attuned to a stop; he will not be listening for our cues, nor will he be likely to stand quietly after the stop.

When you are loping quietly on good ground, the almost simultaneous cues are: pick up on the reins; lean back, dropping your seat deeply into the saddle; and say whoa. If your horse doesn't slide, pay no attention; gather him into a complete stop (this may take several strides) and sit quietly on him for at least 30 seconds. Then, turn around and lope off.

Again issue the cues: ask him, gather him, sit quietly, turn him around, and try again. The response from the horse will vary. He might begin to drop his rear end after only one or two tries; he might require ten.

The point here is that we are trying to set up a situation in which the horse enjoys taking part. A situation that doesn't feel hurried, forced, or pressured, and after which he can relax. If we constantly convey this to him, in a short period of time he will catch on and understand what is coming and prepare for it.

When this happens, we're making headway. He'll almost try to beat us to the stops, and those slide marks will be evidence that we are on the right

112

Photo by Waltenberry

Here's non-pro reiner Jennifer Easton, Stillwater, Minn., stopping her mare, Gilda Glitter.

program. Sliding should get progressively easier for the horse.

Observe the horse and when he is completely comfortable in this maneuver, and when you both feel confident, it's time to increase the speed. Many horses slide best when they are speeded up. When we begin this speeding-up campaign, it is probably advisable to do the stopping while pointing away from the barn or the gate to the training area. Horses are often magnetized by the barn and they will rarely run away from it as fast as they will run towards it. This magnet works on the stops, too. Horses always seem to stop best going down the track away from the barn. It doesn't hurt to take advantage of this characteristic.

This is the basic program to prepare and teach a horse to stop. The work on which we have previously concentrated contributed significantly to the exercises used to progress from a basic stop to a sliding stop. It is easy to understand the importance of collection when we work on soft but aggressive stops.

Remember: Straightness is fundamentally important—it is a prerequisite to a good stop. The horse's body must be straight, so if problems arise, go back to the basics—back to straightness. Be patient and build to speed only as your horse has become proficient and comfortable with the slower stages. Watch him; he'll tell you when he's ready to progress.

12 PLAN YOUR ROUTINE

If we plan our routine, we can always set up situations that allow the horse to gain proficiency in his weak areas.

I'd have to guess that few trainers actually plan their training sessions. To me this is a mistake. It is almost like a third-grade teacher asking her class: "What shall we learn today?" Horses and third-graders have a lot in common, and lesson plans are by no means unnecessary or out of date. We need them.

We have been discussing horse training as a progression of developing skills and facilities. As the horse learns the exercises and maneuvers, they get easier for him, and it is only at this point that we can ask for the next stage of development. Without question the horse tells us in unmistakable language when he is ready to advance, but, of course, we must watch him for the indicators: his willingness, skill, quietness, lack of stress, and his need to be challenged.

Putting a horse on a planned routine has many advantages. The most important: It gives the horse a chance to absorb what he has learned because we are consciously scheduling time for him to learn. It is the rare athlete who can accomplish immediately a new, totally unfamiliar move.

Another advantage to a routine is that it encourages us to teach our horse many things in a single session rather than to drill and drill on a weak spot which would strain his attitude and accomplish little else. If we plan our routine, we can always set up situations that allow the horse to gain proficiency in his weak areas without his anticipation of a problem and bracing against us.

If we as riders and trainers are observant and half awake, we remember our previous session and use it to help plan the next. Consider that no two horses train exactly alike, so the training sessions do not need to be alike. Recognize the individuality in each horse. Do not fit the horse into a rigidly pre-determined pattern; try to figure out what is the best situation through which the individual horse can learn about your ideas. Tailor the program to the needs

As we unsaddle and put our colt away, we'll review how he worked and make mental, or even written, notes. That helps us train according to a plan, instead of haphazardly. Trainers working with 10 to 20 colts every day especially need to make notes.

HORSES

1 CAROLYN
2 BEAUTY
3 BEULAH BURNS
4 LONESOME POLECAT
5 HAIRBREATH HARRY
6 BUCKY
7 BILLY BOY
8 MARYJUANA
9 3 SOCKS
10 4 SOCKS
11 POKEY
12 BOOTS
13 BUBBA
14 PALO GELD
15 Okie Joe Gypsy
16 Okie Joe Princess
17 BLACK BART
18 AGGIE
19 Heidi
20 Critter
21 Rose
22 ALEXIS
23 BUBBLES
24
25
26 BOBCAT
27 LUCKY LADY
28 GOLDEN GIRL
29 SYLVIA
30 NURSE
31 JAMACA
32 LIL DARLIN'
33 SQUIRT

This is a photograph of the chart we use to make daily notes on horses in training. I got the idea from my friend, Thoroughbred trainer Wayne Lukas, who charts the progress of his colts in minute detail.

of the horse.

In fact, during many sessions we shouldn't train at all. A horse gets tired of being pushed, pulled, legged, stopped, turned, and backed. Let him see some fresh country with the least amount of direction. Give him a recess or a field trip. He will return to the barn like a little kid ready for a show-and-tell session with his friends.

Don't train your horse willy-nilly. Plan your work, and work your plan, and don't be afraid to physically write your plan out in tentative form.

I have a close personal friend named Wayne Lukas, one of the world's leading Thoroughbred race horse trainers; he needs no introduction to the horse industry. He personally oversees the training of more than 200 Thoroughbred horses, and he races simultaneously at 5 major tracks in the United States. His horses consistently win millions of dollars each year, and there is a reason why. He takes meticulous care of his horses and plans their training to the nth degree.

The 2-year-olds in training are graded every week and their progress is charted in minute detail. After each day's schooling, the next day's routine is posted. Charts are kept on all horses, and Wayne can get last year's charts out and tell you what any horse did on any given day of his training, race days included.

According to Wayne, it is amazing how much you can learn studying the training charts. He is so right. The important point for us to note is that his

A horse gets tired of always being "in school." Let him see some fresh country . . . take him on a field trip and he'll return to the barn like a little kid ready for a show-and-tell session with his friends.

Photo by Pat Close

horses are trained according to plan. Nothing is done haphazardly, and every routine has its reason and its purpose.

We have discussed how all western training is an exercise in control, but we must decide what we are going to control and where the controls are most needed before a routine or program can be designed.

Let's take a hypothetical case. We have a 2-year-old colt just coming out of the round pen. He has had five to ten saddlings; he'll walk and trot around the round pen, and he has probably been loped a little. We have him in a snaffle and he moves forward willingly. This colt responds a little laterally, but not much. He will not back up, and he stops only half-heartedly. Here's the colt, so what might be our next training session?

This is a hypothetical session, but let's discuss it. First we will walk the colt around for control and calmness. Then we'll acquaint him with head position by asking for his face and rewarding him when he tries.

Next, we may help him position his forelegs and start him following the rein with his feet while walking him in a circle. We want him to learn to step laterally with his inside foreleg; as the inside front foot leaves the ground, we pick up on the inside rein and ask him to move his foot laterally. We're working to direct his feet.

We might then walk him in straight lines and ask for collection. Next, we might introduce him to hindquarter control by walking him in a circle while at the same time moving his hindquarters away from our inside leg, and follow this by moving his rear end a few steps around the forehand. Asking him to stop and stand quietly might be next, and then we might begin working on backing up.

What more could we ask from a colt? We will have had him out for only 20 to 30 minutes, so we will not run the risk of tiring him or boring him. We will not move him out of a walk so we won't confuse, stress, or irritate him, and we won't try to force anything on him that he isn't prepared for and capable of handling.

Best of all, we will have worked on all the parts in a situation where he understood what we were after. We'll leave him in a nice frame of mind, and he'll look forward to tomorrow's lesson, rather than dreading it.

As we unsaddle and put the colt away, we'll review his reactions to our theories and our practice. Maybe he was a little slow in his hindquarter work, or possibly he didn't carry his head straight when we walked in straight lines. Maybe he really caught on to the collection work but hated to take a step backwards. On all these things we make mental (even written) notes and the next day we spend a little more time on them.

We don't need to spend "drilling" time on them, but rather we are patient—allowing the colt the time to absorb our ideas. Possibly two or three times during the session, we go back to the weak spots in order to allow for this absorbing to take place. We'll reissue the cues and try again, and ask—not force—and we'll reward even the slightest evidence of trying. *Remember: There is always a tomorrow with a colt.* We want to be on his time schedule, not our own.

The big thing to consider when planning training sessions is that we are after control—not control of the horse, but control of the parts of the horse. We must quietly direct the parts of the horse first. But be cautious. It is easy, once the colt begins to respond, to arrive at the mistaken idea that he is ready for more challenge and that we have the parts mastered. Stay at the walk and don't jump in over your head. Wait for him.

Putting a horse on a planned routine has many advantages, the most important of which is that it gives the horse a chance to absorb what he has learned, because we are scheduling time for him to learn. If we as riders are observant, we remember our previous session and use it to help plan the next.

Photo by Peter Phinny

Another advantage to a routine is that it encourages us to work on many things in a single session, rather than to repeatedly drill on a weak spot, which would strain the horse's attitude. Here, I am working on this young stallion's turn-around, but I will be careful not to spend too much time before going on to the next lesson.

The amazing thing about bringing a horse along through a routine geared for his individual strengths and weaknesses is that the more you ask from him, the easier it is for him. This colt has progressed nicely because of the program tailored to his individual needs. Here, he's driving quietly out of a roll-back.

It seems to be a good idea during the first four to five sessions at the walk to go through the routine you have established in the same order each session. A horse has an excellent memory and, if we keep the situations the same, he soon finds comfort and shows no confusion in the routine. When his response shows us that he has no trouble doing the movements we ask for, then we can vary the routine and set up new situations to allow him to make better use of his newly acquired skills. Now we can offer him more advanced situations; not more intense situations, just situations that ask him to stretch his ability farther.

The amazing thing about bringing a horse along through a routine geared for his individual strengths and weaknesses is that the more you ask from him under these circumstances, the easier it is for him. Why? Because the horse is beginning to learn to use his body correctly, he is in the process of learning in a pleasant, actually fun, way, and with someone he has learned to trust. As a consequence, he will also develop a softness about his head and neck that is an unmistakably positive attribute of the planned routine training approach; it's a by-product.

Hit-and-miss training sessions are exactly that, and they create difficulties in areas where there never should have been any. The hit-and-miss training programs promote confusion, a lack of confidence by the horse, and therefore tenseness and problems.

So think about what you are doing and what you are going to do, and plan it out, but don't overdo it. There is always a tomorrow; keep it fun for the colt and you'll both enjoy the process. Remember this old saw: Training is a progression and, in order to progress, you must keep things in order, you must get first things first. The first thing to get is control of the parts of the horse in a quiet, orderly manner. In the early stages, your horse will find comfort in a routine.

My wife, Susan, and I constantly talk over the progress and training program we have established for each of our horses. Each horse is an individual, and we regard him as such.

13 AVOIDING DEFENSIVENESS

Most resistance is generated when we interfere with a colt's natural flow, his natural habit, and his natural inclination to do things according to instinct. If we can do away with a problem before it develops, we can school horses.

As a small boy I used to hear stories from my father and our hired hands about horsemen who could do anything with a horse. When individuals who possessed these powers were mentioned, I was all ears, and I couldn't wait to see them in action.

Many were old draft-horse and driving-horse men. They would appear mostly at horse sales, county fairs, and small horse shows. They were practicing horsemen who farmed, ranched, and traded horses. Many of the older men had operated livery stables (livery

I have begun to introduce the sliding stop to this young mare, and here she is bracing a little. But I'll be patient with her because she is fully schooled in the basics of collection. Soon, my cues will make sense to her and she'll find that she can stop comfortably, with less stiffness in her poll and neck. The absolute wrong thing to do would be to pull on her harder. That would cause her to brace even more.

Photo by Peter Phinny

I have been working on this mare's turn-around, and she has begun putting up her defenses, which you can see by her stiff neck and the frazzled look in her eye. If I were to push her and demand even more, I would intensify the problem and I couldn't teach her anything. Instead, I must back off, slow her down, and work at a speed and level of training in which she has total confidence. She has told me that she's not ready to move as fast as I had thought. It's my job to recognize her signals.

Photo by Peter Phinny

outfits were a historical part of America's commercial horse operation). Since these horsemen were in contact with hundreds of horses annually, they were exposed to all the vices and bad habits that a horse could come up with. Also, since all bad habits are the result of trainer ignorance or treatment, they were artists at reclaiming horses. They all tried to buy the spoiled horse as cheaply as possible, work out the kinks, and quickly resell him.

As I think about these men now, I realize that they all had much in common, but the thing that I remember most is that they constantly watched their horses. As a group they were the keenest observers, and they were never in a hurry. They seemed to always be leading a horse or watching while someone else led one. Of course, they nodded wisely as all sages do to add to the mystique of their reputations.

My father hired one of these horsemen to come to our ranch to help with a draft horse that kicked. This horse would kick

A horse's instinctive reaction to fear is flight. When a colt is first saddled and turned loose in the round pen, he speeds around, mentally sorting things out. But since there is no pressure on him, his fear will gradually subside and he will slow down. If, on the other hand, we had forced him to accept too many things at once, we would have increased his fear level even more. **Photo by Peter Phinny**

while being harnessed, and he was definitely dangerous. The old man had a treatment, of course, and it worked. This horse kicked out when the harness fell over his hindquarters. The old horseman's approach was to fill a sack with corncobs and hang it behind the horse's tie stall on a long rope. Then he pulled the sack up and down, and even onto the horse's rear end. He let the horse kick at the harmless bag of corncobs until the horse's fear, and/or resistance, broke down and he didn't care whether or not the sack of corncobs or the harness slapped against him.

This horseman informed us that the first thing to do with a problem horse is to break down his resistance. He was talking above me, but my Dad remembered and he preached it thereafter; the point was and is that any deviation from normal attitude and performance is some form of resistance. Once we develop resistance, it is our problem to deal with, and in any circumstance we are better off without it.

Most resistance is generated when we interfere with a colt's natural flow, his natural habit, and his natural inclination to do things according to instinct. If we can do away with a problem before it develops, we can school horses. I'd much rather do without problems than to have to try to treat them, even if I am able to end up treating them successfully.

Anything we do with a saddle horse is quite obviously based on motion and control of motion. Generally this motion is forward, some of the time lateral, and occasionally backward. Most forward motion is easy to summon; controlling this motion becomes the challenge. Don't forget: The difference between the best and the worst of any performing horse in any event is nothing more than motion control.

Because many trainers force control on their horses, they are far from proficient. They often force this control without any consideration as to how it is going to be accepted by their pupils. If a colt resists, the trainer's objectives are forced on the colt more firmly, and the horse's resistance is then in its developing stage.

This resistance may appear in many different forms. Perhaps the colt will bolt and run away from his treatment. Perhaps he will try to rid himself of the treatment by bucking his rider off. Maybe he'll sull-up and refuse to do anything. He could run backwards or through a fence or obstacle.

The problem and the cause are one and the same; we forced something on him. Ray Hunt says it best when he constantly admonishes his students: "Don't force it on him, offer it to him."

If we offer our program to a colt and allow him to accept it, fairly soon he thinks that it is his idea, and we have cemented a good habit. If he doesn't accept it right off, we find a better way to offer it again. We may have to gift wrap our program, but the secret is to get him to accept and to be happy with the trade. This is horse psychology, and it is a basis for setting up situations to alleviate fears and cure problems.

Defensiveness is probably the most overlooked problem that we encounter in the entire training process. It is so evident that we overlook it and take it as a natural situation or a part of a horse's makeup. We as handlers and trainers are experts at putting a horse on the defensive. The amazing thing is that the horse is able to put up with us, and the tragic thing is that trainers don't recognize defensiveness and do something to eliminate it.

A horse goes on defense when he becomes uncomfortable, and he tells us in unmistakable terms. Our problem is that we don't read the signals that he is waving at us. The horse is trying to tell us that there is something wrong, that he is uncomfortable, and that a change is in order. Our reaction to his defensiveness is probably to use more force, thinking that we can correct the situation.

This force will be manifested by an increase in the use of the leg, rein, or spur, and as a result the horse will do one of two things. First, the problem might become more pronounced or, second, he will develop an additional problem as a result of trying to evade the first problem.

Let's think about this. Why did he become defensive? What forces are at work here?

By nature a horse's instinctive reaction to fear is flight. It is his only means of protecting himself. He doesn't have fangs or claws, and he is not a fighter by nature. Nevertheless, he has been endowed with speed, and he will use it, especially to escape. Don't doubt that if we scare a horse he will try to leave. This is his only real option when we're on his back.

If his defensive attitude is based on fear, he will try to flee from the situation. We then react by wanting to force him to stop or slow down, and our only means is to pull on the reins. If we continue to pull without trying to negate the fear motive, our situation does not improve. We lose the feeling in the horse's mouth, his head position, and his bridle attitude, and you can bet that he'll develop a new problem.

Such a problem might appear as head tossing or gaping (the continuous opening of the mouth), and to top it off, the horse won't forget this experience very easily.

All right, we have established that in this situation the horse wants to leave because he is afraid of something. If we want to remedy this situation, our first priority is to remove the fear motive. We do this by trying to find out what he is afraid of. If he is afraid of punishment, we better quit punishing him and work to get him to establish some trust in us. Believe me, your horse won't trust you if he's afraid of you. The calmness route is never wrong.

When in question, go back to the basics. Do things easily; don't ask for more than he understands, and by all means give him time. Perhaps change his training schedule and routine. He will show you when he feels comfortable. As he softens his resistance, gradually work him back to the point where the trouble all began, and at this juncture he must be happy enough with his situation not to want to leave it.

Defensiveness in a horse takes form in the horse's reaction to punishment itself. If we punish the horse and he fails to understand why, he will become defensive. We also call this bracing. His reactions will vary as to the degree of timing of the punishment. His performance will be erratic. He will be more concerned with the punishment he is getting, or about to get, than with having a nice workout.

The horse may also exhibit a little of the fear motive, but not enough to cause him to run away. The most noticeable of his reactions will be tenseness, and this tenseness will be evident at various points on his body, depending on what he is bracing against.

If we are severe with our hands and punish the horse by pulling and jerking on the reins, the horse will respond with a tenseness in his neck and poll. His neck

Defensiveness is probably the most overlooked problem that we encounter in the entire training process.

Defensiveness in a horse takes form in the horse's reaction to punishment itself. If we punish the horse and he fails to understand why, he will become defensive.

Here, I am demonstrating how a horse will become defensive when he is confused. I've asked this colt to try to roll back over his hocks, but I did not issue the proper signals to prepare him for the maneuver. Not only has he stiffened up in his mouth, poll, and neck, but his eyes also reflect confusion and worry.

will rise, his neck muscles will become tense and hard, he will elevate his nose, and hold his head in a rigid, nose-up position. If this is the case, he is trying to protect and brace himself against another pull which he feels will soon be coming.

With his head and neck in this position, his stride will be shortened and he will lose all cadence and rhythm in his lope. His stride will be choppy and the stiffness which accompanies it will be unmistakably felt. This is a manifestation of defensiveness, so don't overlook it.

I often see riders punish their horses with both bit and spur. They suddenly stick the horse with a spur, causing him to jump forward, and when he does, they suddenly snatch or jerk him. No question that this will put a horse on the

defense, but his reactions to this punishment will be varied.

You can bet that his head will be elevated and his lower jaw braced or tensed. His face will approach the horizontal, and his primary concern will be to prepare himself for what he thinks is coming next. There is no softness in this horse, no alertness, no inquisitiveness, only pure self-defense—survival. His mental facilities in this stressed situation will not allow him to think, concentrate, learn, or absorb what the trainer would like to teach him.

The very best way to solve the defensiveness problem is to eliminate the offensive training tactics that are responsible for it. Remove the cause in order to effect a cure. You cannot find anything more valuable than softness, observation, consideration, and infinite patience in schooling a horse, and especially when schooling for the basics. A strong foundation is an absolute must, and don't be afraid to sacrifice for it. Time means nothing; take the time necessary and wait for him to indicate when to advance.

Confusion plays a significant role in this subject of defensiveness. A horse will become defensive when he becomes confused, and many trainers consistently confuse their horses. As previously mentioned, some riders will alternately spur and jerk a horse. The horse is spurred to move forward and then jerked for doing it. No matter which way he moves under cue, he is punished for it. He won't take much of this.

We see riders, especially cutters, stick a spur in a horse's shoulder in order to move his front end away from the spur. Actually what happens is almost the opposite. When the spur strikes the horse, he will immediately become tense in the area where he was struck, and his head and neck will move in the same direction to brace against it.

In other words, the horse will stiffen up on the side the rider wants him to move away from. The poor horse then gets severely pulled in the new direction and spurred again for not doing it fast enough. This confuses the horse, and his reaction to it has to be one of extreme nervousness.

In this frame of mind, the horse's performance potential will be severely impaired. The horse simply won't understand. With the wrong cues and the wrong timing, how could he be expected to do it right? This is not much more than common sense.

We witness barrel racers competing on horses with tie-downs and gag snaffles. A gag snaffle is good for only one thing, and that is to raise a horse's head, because it pressures the horse's poll; at the same time, it works off the corners of the mouth. These horses are run through the barrel pattern with their heads tied down and, at the same time, pulled up with the gag. I call this confusion. We see it often and it is amazing to me what horses are willing to put up with.

Anger will also put a horse on the defensive and it can be a catalyst for trainer abuse if it is not dealt with intelligently. Many horses have a short fuse and become agitated when they are misused or mishandled. These horses try to do something about it.

First, they try to rid themselves of the problem. Some, particularly stallions, are shorter fused than others and will react in no uncertain terms. They will buck, stampede, kick, slam themselves into a fence, manifest any number of reactions, and in the process they will be completely out of control. Needless to say, we definitely have no mental contact with them at this time.

Don't be confused about this aggression, however, because it is definitely defensive. It is a reaction to a trainer's, or handler's, mishandling. So our first priority in schooling this horse is to find out why this problem has been created. Again and again, remove the cause.

Defensiveness has always been a problem with all horse trainers, and many, probably the biggest percentage of them, fail to recognize it even when it strikes them in the face. Sometimes when trainers do recognize defensiveness, they misread it and treat it as if it were some sort of stubbornness, meanness, or, what I hear over and over again, "bull-headedness." This is like the vet treating a horse for navicular when all he had was thrush.

We'll all be farther ahead in our training programs if we give the horse the benefit of the doubt and take a close look at how we are trying to get our points across to the horse. We need to diagnose our problems accurately.

Another cause of defensiveness that we should try to avoid is over-training. If a horse becomes bored or tired, he may very well exhibit signs of defensiveness. He may develop an I-don't-give-a-damn attitude and become unresponsive. The spur loses its effect. His mouth becomes dead. He doesn't care and he shows it.

This is the worst kind of defensiveness because the horse does eventually give up if he is not treated fairly. He simply won't try because he can't gain any self-confidence. The rider always seems to arrange for his defeat. Continually guard against over-training and asking for more than the horse understands or is capable of giving.

The most important idea in this book is again appropriate: "Watch your horse!" He will show you what is working well, and what is not. It is up to all of us, as trainers, to make the adjustments.

You cannot find anything more valuable than softness, observation, consideration, and infinite patience in schooling a horse, and especially when schooling for the basics.

14 PROFILE: JACK BRAINARD

Jack and Susan Brainard raise and train between 25 and 30 performance-bred colts and fillies every year.

"Things were simpler when I was a kid. Slower perhaps, and easier to live with. We rode or drove horses most of the time, and even after there were quite a few cars in the country, when we'd meet a neighbor on the road we'd whoa up and visit. It might be below zero, but we still took the time to say howdy, maybe have a smoke together, and swap news. Today you meet a friend on the road, and if you even have time for recognition it will be no more than a quick wave, and you're both long gone. Damn if I didn't like the old ways better, because I can't see what we are gaining by not sparing some time to talk a little."

Spike Van Cleve
40 Years' Gatherin's

Jack Brainard and his Diamond B Ranch in Gainesville, Tex., echo his late friend Spike Van Cleve's sentiment. There is a sense of timelessness in the breeding and training program Jack has developed. No one punches the clock, and everyone works until the job's done. It is a team concept with the boss and the young apprentices working side by side. They don't seem to lose sight of the real value and pleasure that a "handling" horse can give a man when he throws a leg over the saddle.

Although Jack had worked with horses on his father's ranch, his interest in Quarter Horses traces its roots to the Goodrich Ranch in Lampasas, Tex., during his Army days when he was stationed at Camp Hood. The Goodrich

One of the Brainards' horses, Dog Patch Doc, tied for second place in the 1984 NRHA Futurity in Columbus, Ohio, and won the championship in senior reining at the 1986 AQHA World Show in Oklahoma City. He's shown here at the NRHA Futurity with Don Flohr, one of Jack's former apprentices, in the saddle. **Photo by Harold Campton**

Ranch had Starway P-506 and George Hancock, plus several mares that had AQHA numbers below 200. It was on this ranch where he had the chance to work with Glen Chism, whom Jack still considers one of the greatest horsemen he has ever known.

After his discharge Jack returned to his home in Iowa and bought his first Quarter Horse. He then began to rodeo, primarily roping calves. During these early years Jack worked for Leo Cremer of Big Timber, Mont., who at the time was the biggest and best rodeo producer in America. Cremer also had a band of mares that he had purchased from Hank Weiscamp and Warren Shoemaker. In 1947 Jack ended up buying those mares and also a stud Cremer had—a King Ranch-bred horse. Jack has been breeding horses ever since.

Jack then began working as a trainer for some people in Wisconsin, and he has been training horses for a living since

For several years Jack was in the rodeo-producing business as a co-owner of Rodeos Inc.

Jack on the stallion Flying Jim (by Jim Minnick by Norfleet) on his Dad's Iowa ranch in 1946.

then. His experience in the AQHA can be traced to the breed's early show records. He was responsible for taking the first Quarter Horses to Wisconsin and for making the first AQHA Champion in the Upper Midwest, a mare named Ponzell. She was by a horse named Pondie and out of Shelly's Cricket.

Jack was one of the original four people who organized the Iowa Quarter Horse Association and one of the four or five who organized the Upper Midwest Quarter Horse Association (Iowa, Minnesota, and South Dakota). He was also the second president of the Minnesota Quarter Horse Association. In 1966 Jack Brainard was one of the original group that organized the National Reining Horse Association; he served as one of the original directors when the first board convened in 1967.

Jack trained Outer's Stubby, by Baker's Oklahoma Star, the 1957 AQHA Honor Roll Reining Horse. He then moved to Rochester, Minn., and established the Diamond B Ranch. (In the late '70s he moved his operation to its current location in Gainesville, Texas.) It was while living in Rochester that he became involved in the rodeo-producing business as a co-owner of Rodeos Inc. This company became noted for its tremendous stock, particularly its bucking horses. Rodeos Inc. had the distinction of owning horses winning the title of best bronc at the National Finals Rodeo four different times.

When the Nixon administration established the U.S. Horse Industry Advisory Committee, Secretary of Agriculture Earl Butz appointed 15 members, including Jack. This appointment required meetings with the secretary and undersecretary in Washington every four months. He held his position on this committee until it was disbanded.

Jack was a
member of the
U.S. Horse
Industry Advisory
Committee.

This 1955 photo shows Jack on his stallion Bali Bob as a 3-year-old at the Wisconsin State Fair.
Photo by Gerber

Jack holds a judge's card in several associations, and is shown here judging the finals of the American Horse Shows Association stock seat medal finals in Santa Barbara, Calif., in the '70s.

A 1946 photo of Jack on Bar Hug in Fort Davis, Texas. He had the chance to help start this horse with Glen Chism, whom Jack considers one of the greatest horsemen he has ever known.

Jack began judging horses in 1948, and judged cuttings before the NCHA was even established. In 1952 he began judging Quarter Horses and to date he has judged longer than any other active judge in the AQHA. He also served on the rules committee (western division) of the American Horse Shows Association, and he has carried his judge's card in six divisions of this association.

Jack's experience has not been limited; he judges Paints, POAs, Appaloosas, palominos, mules, draft horses, and NCHA cuttings and NRHA reinings. He has judged every major show in the United States and most of them twice. He has judged the Fort Worth Fat Stock Show seven times.

Jack Brainard is one of the very few contemporary horsemen who has a working acquaintance with, and knowledge of, every family of Quarter Horses, having ridden the get of the foundation sires. The Diamond B Ranch breeding program is a product of this experience and of more than 30 years of selecting

Jack reining on Yeller Hi Life at Denver's National Western Stock Show in 1964.

stallion and broodmare crosses. His training program, which is so integrally linked to the breeding program, has developed from Jack's incessant addiction to pure and unfettered movement in a finished horse, and to the lack of mental stress which makes this possible and which insures a horse's longevity in the show ring.

The major portion of the current Diamond B Ranch broodmare band, carefully cared for and managed by Jack's wife, Susan, includes daughters and granddaughters of King, Poco Bueno, Mr. Joe Glo, Okie Leo, Wimpy, and Bali Bob. Other mares in the band include King Ranch mares as well as mares with Hobby Horse, Blondy's Dude, and

At the 1988 NRHA Futurity, Kim Diercks rode one of Jack's horses, Bubba Looie, to win the open division of the $1,000 added championship novice horse class. Jack and Susan are holding some of the awards.

Photo by Waltenberry

At the Minnesota State Fair one year, Jack won the reining horse stake on Mano's Buster.

Photo by Alexander

Parker's Trouble pedigrees.

It is no accident that these broodmares closely trace their heritage to the very foundation of the Quarter Horse registry. Jack, through firsthand experience, has ridden, trained, and shown horses with these bloodlines. They are proven commodities, producing foals on whose ability he can depend, year after year.

The stallion battery (none of whom stand to outside mares) has included Diamond B Okie, a son of Okie Leo out of a daughter of Poco Bueno; Poco Pretty Boy, a son of Poco Bueno out of a daughter of Jessie James; and Dog Patch Doc, a son of Doc's Lynx out of a daughter of Okie Leo. Dog Patch Doc tied for second place in the 1984 NRHA Futurity, and became the AQHA World Champion Senior Reining Horse in 1986.

Jack, with friend and partner Burdette Johnson, owned the now-deceased Mr. Joe Glo, an AQHA Champion and sire of

This is Jack's son Jody, riding one of Jack's horses, Freckled Like Dad, at the '88 NRHA Futurity where he placed ninth in the limited open division. Jody operates his own training business in Green Bay, Wisconsin. Freckled Like Dad, by Colonel Freckles and out of Miss Annie Dee Bar, is being used in Jack's breeding program.   **Photo by Waltenberry**

NRHA Futurity and Super Stakes winners.

Unlike many breeders, Jack will not even price his colts until they are started 2-year-olds, beginning their careers. The mares are pasture bred, they foal in the open, and the foals spend their first two years of life outside on the Texas range where they can run and develop naturally. Jack claims that "the best health program and the cheapest is a good feeding program." Therefore, his colts receive good grain in addition to hay and forage throughout their early years of freedom.

Beginning in the spring, Jack and Susan separate the 2-year-olds into groups of between eight and twelve, starting one group at a time in the training pen with intervals of about 60 days between groups. "We never know which colts are our best because we've always got groups at different stages of training," Jack explains. "The ones we take to the futurities invariably come from the youngest group, the last group started, because most of the others will have been sold by futurity time. But this is okay; we feel we're still in good shape with our own entries because these colts have been uniformly good athletes. We're really proud of 'em."

With an approach similar to that of an NFL coach, Jack enjoys developing talented riders as well as horses.

Beginning approximately in March, the Diamond B training pens resemble an unveiling at an auto show. Jack, accompanied by a young apprentice or two, shows the started 2-year-olds to futurity-winning trainers and non-pros who come from as far away as California and Georgia. Diamond B horses end up in all walks of western life, from all the show-ring events to ranch and rodeo work.

For years Jack has had the reputation for putting a solid foundation on his colts, a foundation on which trainers and showmen are eager to supply their personal finish. Diamond B Ranch colts regularly end up in the World Championship Snaffle Bit Futurity (for reined cow horses) and the NRHA Futurity, as well as in the Texas futurities and in other major events.

Probably the greatest influence in the last 15 years on Jack's training program can be traced to his friendship and association with Tom Dorrance and Ray Hunt. Jack's horses work without stress in the Dorrance/Hunt tradition. They perform out of willingness and trust, not through fear and intimidation.

Even though Jack and his team school between 25 and 30 horses, each horse is regarded as an individual and is allowed to develop on his own timetable. "We don't want 'em to be simply a futurity horse, or a derby horse; we want 'em to last, to have an active show career after the futurity or the derby, or whatever event comes first in their careers. Here again, we believe that if prospects are developed without intimidation and fear, they'll have a better chance of staying fresh and eager for years. That's what we want."

The team concept is a fundamental element in the Diamond B operation. Susan has responsibility for the mares and the young colts. Jack and his assistants ride and train. But Jack is the coach and general manager. Over the years he has influenced trainers and given young aspirants opportunities to work with him and for him. It is a rare opportunity, indeed, when a raw young rider and would-be trainer can have the chance to ride 25 to 30 young horses with the athletic ability and breeding possessed by the Diamond B colts.

Through Jack's association with one of his proteges, Larry Kasten, director of the Equine Studies Program at the University of Wisconsin/River Falls, he has hired several student apprentices who are now active in the NRHA. Among them are Don Flohr, Tom Pierson, and Kim Diercks. Jack's son Jody, who has a training facility with his wife, Linda, in Green Bay, Wis., is a tough and active NRHA competitor, as is NRHA Futurity winner Craig Johnson, who also began his horse show career with Jack's help. Other apprentices have included Al Peaslee, Jerry Stjkskal, Pat Fitzgerald, Ed Tichenor, Roger Mork, and Butch Stein.

With an approach similar to that of an NFL coach, Jack enjoys developing talented riders as well as horses. Even with natural ability, a person requires seasoning to become a competitor. A good coach has to stick with apprentices even when they go off pattern, tense up in the show ring, or don't prepare their horses properly—any of the mistakes young riders can make. Jack has shown an admirable balance between demanding excellence and refusing to pull the rug out from under an assistant's feet.

For Jack, the horse business and training of horses has a broad context; he will never escape his ranch background and the realization that his program isn't built on just one horse. His association with horses began as a small boy influenced by his grandfather and his father, and life on their ranch.

The Diamond B Ranch philosophy evidences a heritage linked to the old ways—a way of life that relied on the horse. Jack and Susan Brainard's horses come with a heritage systematically developed from the proven foundation sires in the Quarter Horse registry. Perhaps Spike Van Cleve's simple words from *40 Years' Gatherin's* might have as easily been spoken by Jack: "I am a horseman. I was raised with them, have lived with them all my life, and I hope I'll die with them. I've known a lot of good ones and a few bad ones."

—*Peter Phinny*

134

About the Author —Peter Phinny

Peter Tyler Phinny, author and free-lance writer.

Photo by Molly Phinny

Peter Phinny graduated from Wesleyan University in 1972. Although his primary interest is the writing of novel-length fiction, he has been actively involved in writing within the field of equine journalism. In addition to the *Western Horseman*, his articles have appeared in *The Blood-Horse, The Quarter Horse Journal*, and other horse publications. He is the co-author, with Jack Brainard, of a previous book entitled *Training the Reined Horse*, published in 1977 by A.S. Barnes & Company.

Phinny lives with his wife, Molly, and stepchildren, Christopher and Emily, on a small farm in Cedar, Mich., where he raises and sells Quarter Horses. He maintains close proximity to the horses and events about which he writes by also schooling and showing his horses. Phinny is a non-pro in the National Reining Horse Association. "I'm only an occasional competitor," he says, "in what must be considered the minor leagues of the NRHA, but I do love my horses."

Peter Phinny has had both a personal and a professional friendship with Jack Brainard since approximately 1970 when he first attended a clinic in which Jack, then associated with the University of Wisconsin at River Falls, instructed.

Publisher's Note: Both Peter Phinny and Jack Brainard would like to thank Craig Johnson for allowing his training track in Gainesville, Tex., to be used for taking the pictures in this book. They also appreciate the help of Kim Diercks, Jack's assistant trainer. Since the photos were taken, Kim has moved back to her home in Coloma, Wis., to operate her own training facility.

Peter stopping his favorite reining horse, Grand River Jim.

Photo by Duane Zielkowski

Western Horseman Magazine

Colorado Springs, Colorado

The Western Horseman Magazine, established in 1936, is the world's leading horse publication.
For subscription information and a list of other Western Horseman books, contact:
Western Horseman Magazine, P.O. Box 7980, Colorado Springs, CO 80933-7980; ph. 719-633-5524.

Distributed to the book trade by
Texas Monthly Press, Inc.
P.O. Box 1569, Austin, TX 78767-1569
Ph. 800-288-3288